As GOD IS
WE MAY
BECOME

As God is WE MAY BECOME

A BIBLICAL PERSPECTIVE ON THE PLAN OF SALVATION

BY STEVEN C. COLWELL

Horizon Publishers
Springville, Utah

ISBN 13: 978-0-88290-805-7
ISBN 10: 0-88290-805-7
Order # C3008
e. 1

Published by Horizon Publishers, an imprint of Cedar Fort, Inc.,
925 N. Main, Springville, UT, 84663
Distributed by Cedar Fort, Inc. www.cedarfort.com

LIBRARY OF CONGRESS CATALOGING-IN-PUBLICATION DATA

Colwell, Steven C.
  As God is we may become / by Steven C. Colwell.
    p. cm.
  Includes bibliographical references.
  ISBN 0-88290-805-7
  1. Church of Jesus Christ of Latter-day Saints--Doctrines.
  2. Mormon Church--Doctrines. 3. Christian life--Mormon authors.
  I. Title.
  BX8675.C65 2006
  230'.9332--dc22

                              2006002145

Cover design by Nicole Williams
Cover design © 2006 by Lyle Mortimer
Printed in the United States of America

10   9   8   7   6   5   4   3   2   1

Printed on acid-free paper

DEDICATION

To my wonderful friend and spiritual brother Steven Bende. In a short period of time, we developed an astounding relationship. His influence upon me reaches far deeper than he can imagine. The first time I was privileged to be in his presence, there awakened an aspect of my soul that had long lay dormant. The effect of his friendship upon me caused a self-examination that has allowed me to achieve what I once could only envision. He has challenged me most mightily, yet unobtrusively. He is a man of tremendous intellect and knowledge, humility and compassion, as well as enthusiasm, benevolence, and love. Though he would deny it, he is surely one of the world's greatest thinkers. And to crown his accomplishments, he is the embodiment of a true gentleman. I hold him in the highest esteem and regard.

His friendship is one of the greatest treasures with which I will ever be blessed. I am unable to express the depth of my gratitude for his instruction, encouragement, and influence. I am eternally grateful for our brotherhood and am eternally in his debt. May God bless him most richly, and may our friendship and association transcend space and time.

TABLE OF CONTENTS

PREFACE

Come now, and let us reason together, saith the Lord: though your sins be as scarlet they shall be as white as snow; though they be red like crimson, they shall be as wool.

—Isaiah 1:18

Whom shall he teach knowledge? and whom shall he make to understand doctrine? them that are weaned from the milk, and drawn from the breasts. For precept must be upon precept, precept upon precept; line upon line, line upon line; here a little, and there a little.

—Isaiah 28:9–10

I have yet many things to say unto you, but ye cannot bear them now. Howbeit when he, the Spirit of truth, is come, he will guide you into all truth: for he shall not speak of himself; but whatsoever he shall hear, that shall he speak: and he will shew you things to come.

—John 16:12–13

The above verses from the Old Testament and New Testament, perhaps more than any other found in the scriptures, set the tone for this book. They establish a pattern of thought, revelation, and confirmation that lead to enlightenment. Enlightenment on a single point of truth that gives way to another single point of truth that continues line upon line, precept upon precept, truth upon truth until all truths coalesce into the ultimate single truth. Through revelation, confirmation, and enlightenment, we will come to a sure knowledge that God our Heavenly Father, Jesus Christ, and the Holy Ghost are separate and singular entities with the same mission. That their mission is for us to realize that God is perfect love; that Christ performed the greatest act of love and compassion in all history by His atoning sacrifice; that the Holy Ghost is the revelator of truth, peace and comfort; and that in His perfect love for us, His children, God would grant us His greatest blessing.

Simply stated, His greatest blessing and the singular and ultimate truth in which all other truths are embodied is this: as God is, we may become.

As bold a statement as that is, as shocking as it may seem, as contrary to what our preconceived notion of God and our relationship to Him is, nonetheless, it is still the truth. It is neither far-fetched nor blasphemous, neither absurd nor profane. It is simply the ultimate truth.

As stated in Isaiah 1:18, we are to use our God-given reasoning power to unite with His power of reasoning. His power of reasoning is given to us not only through the recorded inspirational revelations of the prophets but also through personal revelation. God would not have us blindly follow Him, although that is better than not following at all, but He would have us know the who, what, when, where, why, and how of His doctrine, so our knowledge may be total. He would have us choose through the exercise of our agency for ourselves; He will let us learn from the consequences of our choices.

If we but allow it, if we wean ourselves from the milk, these verses will speak directly to our spirit and unfold verity, beauty, and peace of such magnitude and importance that our lives will be changed for all time and eternity in accordance with God's desire.

As the Lord has said, "Come now, and let us reason together" Isaiah 1:18). That is exactly what we will do throughout this book. As He has set the parameters of our education, we will learn "precept upon precept; line upon line, line upon line; here a little, and there a little" (Isaiah 28:10).

Let us now follow the commandment of God, the direction He would have our learning follow and the confirmation of its truth through the promptings of the Holy Ghost, by examining God's plan for our happiness and eternal salvation.

ACKNOWLEDGMENTS

The help of the following persons is most deeply appreciated. They have given of their time, talents, and energy to assist me in numerous areas during the development of this book.

First, I would like to thank Cindy Morris. A woman of amazing abilities, she unhesitatingly agreed to peruse my first manuscript. She endured the hardship of plowing through the first draft and added wonderful comments and grammatical corrections. Her honesty gave impetus to my tentative undertaking.

Next, I would like to thank Harry and Nancy Haun. At my personal request, they read my semifinished manuscript from a most critical point of view and added thoroughly appropriate comments and ideas.

Paul Smith was invaluable with his technical contributions in bringing about the physical manifestations of my research.

Richard Wilson consented to be my home editor and theologian, an endeavor he fulfilled with exceeding aptitude. His wonderful gift and depth of spiritual knowledge and ability to discern the pattern and intention of my thoughts and writing gave him the insight to correctly critique my work. He recognized my errors and pointed out when I needed deeper analysis and explanation, or when some passage needed to be totally reworked. He was a joy to work with, and he devoted significant time and effort to assist me. I had high hopes for what I thought he could do. I had no idea that he would surpass those hopes so beautifully. He assisted me with compassion and tenderness, and our sessions going over his critiques of the manuscript blessed me with more than simply practical solutions to certain difficulties. Our time spent together put the gospel in a working perspective, and more important, it blessed us with a peace and joy that can only be found in doing the Lord's work.

I thank my daughter, Vanessa, for her belief in me and for her assistance when I began to write. She gave me encouragement as well as advice.

She was a valuable help in writing the first draft of this book. Her insight, intelligence, and love were most touching.

And, of the greatest importance, I thank my wife, Charlotte. She supported me unwaveringly through the late work hours required by my schedule and the massive time needed to complete this endeavor. She never criticized or complained when I spent time that could have been spent doing the myriad things necessary to marriage and family. She never complained when attention to other practical matters might have taken precedence. She was patient, understanding, and encouraging, and without her, none of this would have come to fruition.

INTRODUCTION

I belong to The Church of Jesus Christ of Latter-day Saints, commonly known as the Mormon Church or, among its members, the Church. I originally wrote this book for those who are not members of my faith. It was intended to be a primer of sorts, a treatment of basic gospel principles.

When the rough draft was completed, I asked a few friends to evaluate the manuscript. Their reaction took me by surprise.

Among those who read the first treatment were lifelong members of the Church. Based upon their comments, I realized that this work would be valuable not only to the general public, potential members, and new members but to all members of the Church. The effect of this work upon those to whom it was initially presented astonished me. It seems that a new light was shed on certain gospel principles, and my friends came away with a greater knowledge, understanding, depth of spirituality, and appreciation for the plan of salvation.

As delineated in this book, the Bible explains God's plan for us. However, it does not present the plan in a simple, clear, and concise manner. All the principles and ordinances for salvation are there, but they are spread through various books of the Old Testament and New Testament and are rather poorly linked.

The beauty of the Book of Mormon, Another Testament of Jesus Christ, is the clarity it unfolds to this wonderful plan. It is succinct and forthright. It testifies of God, the Father; His Son, Jesus Christ; and the Holy Ghost. It testifies of Their mission and purpose and what we are to do. In fact, the Book of Mormon gives God's plan several names, including the plan of salvation, God's plan for our happiness, plan of the Eternal Father, plan of redemption, plan of the great Creator, plan of God, and so forth.

This book will use the various names of God's plan interchangeably, with each term used to give the clearest reference to what is being discussed at the time.

Sadly, most of the world has failed to recognize the Book of Mormon, Another Testament of Jesus Christ, as scripture. There is also an underlying, though unfounded, belief that the Book of Mormon is meant to replace the Bible. That is not the case. The Book of Mormon goes hand in hand with the Bible and testifies of the Bible's truthfulness and the divinity of Christ.

I intend my book to not only explain the plan of salvation, along with where we came from, why we are here, and where we are going, but just as important, to bridge the gap and be a defining link between the Bible and the Book of Mormon. My hope is that this work establishes a bridge that will help everyone to cross between the two books of scripture, come to a deeper understanding of them both, and discover their true and united purpose. My hope is for all readers to receive personal revelation and obtain a greater depth of spiritual understanding.

Concerning the scriptures, the Bible used for reference in this book is the King James Version. Though some find modern translations of this version easier to read because of the use of present-day language, many modern translations of this masterful work sadly omit many precious facts, truths, and statements, and remove themselves by another generation from the purest transcript we have of the revealed word given in ancient time. Even the King James Version, after multiple translations and through accident as well as deliberation, has lost numerous true and key elements of the teachings of Christ and His doctrines of salvation

There are many phrases throughout this book that will be unfamiliar to those not of the Mormon faith. A phrase is a terse, pithy statement that stands for an entire concept, and many phrases throughout this book are unique to The Church of Jesus Christ of Latter-day Saints and the Book of Mormon. Examples include moral agency, premortal existence, Godhead, eternal marriage, and the celestial, terrestrial, and telestial kingdoms. My hope is my use of phrases not common outside the Church will facilitate the understanding of the gospel principles being discussed.

There will also be some reiteration of certain principles through various chapters. It is because of their importance and unifying nature with the topic currently being treated that I repeat them.

I have written this book with the sincere hope and desire that others will have revealed to them the truths that I have been blessed to receive and to have the blessings of heaven poured upon them with uncounted measure.

In His infinite wisdom, our Heavenly Father instituted a plan whereby we may return to His presence. The purpose of the Bible and the Book of Mormon is to instruct us in God's will. His plan and desire is that one day we may come back home to Him. Our return to Him is based upon our faith and willingness to recognize His character and the manner in which He runs His kingdom. It was through Joseph Smith, the founding prophet of The Church of Jesus Christ of Latter-day Saints, that Christ's church was restored. Joseph Smith penned a wonderful statement concerning the character of God, found in the *Teachings of the Prophet Joseph Smith* (hereafter referred to as *Teachings*), "In the beginning, the head of the Gods called a council of the Gods; and they came together and concocted a plan to create the world and people it. When we begin to learn this way, we begin to learn the only true God, and what kind of a being we have got to worship. Having a knowledge of God, we begin to know how to approach him, and how to ask so as to receive an answer. When we understand the character of God, and know how to come to him, he begins to unfold the heavens to us, and to tell us all about it. When we are ready to come to him, he is ready to come to us" (349–50).

Our Heavenly Father's plan for our happiness and eternal salvation is based on His love for us. He wants us to enjoy the majesty of all His creations for all eternity. He wants us to have all He has. He wants us to return to live with Him in exaltation and glory. In His wisdom, He knows what we must do. In His love, He knows that there is little value in bondage, and we must choose for ourselves and either reap the rewards or suffer the consequences of our actions.

Of course, returning to His presence means we must have already lived with Him. To understand His plan for our salvation and come to a knowledge of where we came from, why we are here, and where we are going, we must examine several stages that led us away from our life with Him and will ultimately lead us back to exaltation and eternal life with Him once again.

The basic tenets of his plan for our salvation are:

1. We needed to be physically separated from God and the memory of our former life with Him and His plan so that we could exercise the first principle of the gospel, which is faith in God and the Lord Jesus Christ.

2. We needed a mortal body. Certain experiences can only be had physically, and learning can take place more rapidly.

3. We needed to live in a world of choices and evil influences so that

we could exercise our moral agency in accordance with God's will.

4. Our Heavenly Father would provide His commandments and instructions through the written word and His prophets. This would occur from the days of Adam through the second coming of Christ and until the world becomes celestialized.

5. We would be provided a Savior who would atone for our sins.

6. We must repent of our sins and transgressions.

7. We must be baptized according to the standard He set forth. Baptism must be performed by an authorized administrator commissioned by God.

8. We must receive the gift of the Holy Ghost by the laying on of hands from one of God's authorized representatives.

9. We must endure in faithful righteousness to the end of our days.

Germane to God's plan is that we realize we are actually His progeny. That we are God's children is not an idle statement, nor is it symbolic or figurative. The scriptures are a cornucopia of verses that attest to the fact that we are the actual children of our Heavenly Father.

We read in Romans 8:16–17, "The Spirit itself beareth witness with our spirit, that we are the children of God: And if children, then heirs; heirs of God, and joint-heirs with him, that we may be also glorified together."

These verses explain that the Spirit, or the Holy Ghost, is telling us by bearing His witness to our spirit that we are truly God's children. Paul, the author of the epistle to the Romans, states that if we are His children then we are truly heirs to what has been promised Christ. We are to be joint-heirs with Jesus! We are to inherit the kingdom of God. All that is His. All the heavens, worlds, and creations brought into existence by His hands. Worlds without end and posterity without number. That we may be glorified with Christ means we might rule and reign as does He. We may be exalted as He is exalted.

That we are God's children is reiterated time and again in scripture. It is set forth in the Old Testament and the New Testament. It is stated so often for a specific purpose—so that we get it. So that we understand it. So that we will gain a sure knowledge of it. So that we recognize it for what it is: a vital and crucial fact pertaining to understanding the plan of salvation and our exaltation.

We are taught this truth, that we are actually and literally His spirit children, so that we may have a proper and accurate perspective on all aspects of our eternal life and existence. We dwelt with our Heavenly Father prior to our mortal birth, and we have the opportunity to live with our Father when we pass beyond mortality. Do we have an actual father of our flesh and bones? Of course. Do we have a father of our spirits? Beyond any shadow of a doubt, Yes!

Your own heart tells you this is so. Is not the ultimate desire of all believers to "go to heaven"? Is not heaven the residence of God our Father? To want to go to heaven is to want to return home and dwell with Him once more. That is His greatest desire for us.

As a small example of our premortal family unit and what we can expect when we return home once again, He has provided us the paradigm of the family. Our mortal family is but a type of eternity. It is a unit of parents and offspring working together in love and harmony for the sake of each other. And it is family helping family with the same desire. Of course, most families fall quite short of this idyllic picture, but we must keep in mind that we are here to learn to love in progressively greater degrees and grow in all other areas in commensurate manner.

The Father of our spirits has given us His love, and His love is perfect. His desires are perfect. He would have us receive everything that is His. If He wished anything less, He would cease to be perfect, and therefore, He would cease to be God. Fortunate for us, that is not the case.

He will show us the way to return to Him. He will also show us the how and the why. A perfect being would not let us wander aimlessly, without direction and under the total influence of the evil one. We will be guided by Divinity along the path that leads back to His presence.

SECTION I:

A GENERAL OVERVIEW OF GOD'S PLAN FOR OUR
HAPPINESS AND SALVATION: WHERE WE CAME FROM,
WHY WE ARE HERE, AND WHERE WE ARE GOING

chapter one

THE FOUNDATION,
MIRACLES, AND FAITH

I have carried the memory with me throughout my life. I was a young child of perhaps four years of age. As I recall that morning in 1954, I was in the front yard sitting on my tricycle. Across the street, the fronds of tall palm trees of monstrous height moved by an imperceptible breeze. The sky was blue as only a clear blue Southern California sky of that era could be. And to crown this most beautiful of days, scattered white clouds, not too many and not too few, lazed about in pastoral grace and splendor. The temperature was not too hot or too cold, and the sun had that pleasing warmth that soothes the skin but promises not to drive away the pleasure.

I remember the beauty of that day, a day that defines perfection: no noise came from nearby traffic or the propeller-driven planes that occasionally penetrated the stillness. The morning was wrapped in the comforting embrace of pure peace. I can close my eyes and recall that morning with absolute clarity, as if I were viewing a still photograph. And yet, in the midst of one of the most splendid days to bless this earth, I was frozen with a feeling, an impression that shaped the rest of my life. *I don't belong here.*

It was as simple and as clear as that. Though I was aware of the exquisite beauty and overwhelming peace of the day, I did not belong here.

It was not that I felt I did not belong to the neighborhood, or my parents, or relatives, or anything that defined life, as I knew it. It was that I did not belong to this earth. It was not a frightening feeling, nor was it unsettling. It was as if something intrinsic, long understood and long forgotten, was unveiled for a brief few minutes. I experienced no promptings to action or feelings of why I did not belong here, where I should go, or what I should do. Just the knowledge that something seemed to be at odds with how things are supposed to be and accompanied by a sad resignation to that fact.

That seems a rather peculiar feeling to come over a four year old. I had a loving family, and although far from rich, we lived comfortably on

3

my father's earnings as a police officer. We did not lack the necessities, and we were beginning to enjoy a few extras. At that age, we rarely notice the discomforts of scarcity, even if they do exist. But such was not our case. We were as comfortable as anybody else in the neighborhood. So for this overwhelming feeling of "I don't belong here" to be experienced on such a core level at such an early age and to have such an effect upon me was an enigma for almost forty years.

Thankfully, after several decades, I discovered why that particular feeling occurred; the answer also explained many subsequent occasions of pure intrinsic knowledge, associated thoughts, feelings, and questions related to that initial revelation. The answer came not by logic, although the answers were logical, nor by intellectual exercise, although they could have been. They were answered by the Holy Spirit.

If we are to find the truth in our quest to understand God's plan for our happiness and salvation and become as is our Heavenly Father, we need to answer the questions: Where did we come from? Why are we here? Where are we going?

It is imperative that we establish a firm foundation. If our foundation is strong enough, it will withstand all queries and arguments. We may always return to it as a sound base and a safe harbor from which to reflect upon and take comfort in what we have learned and then proceed toward our next exploration. In time, we will learn that all experiences are spiritual. Work, play, church, love, business, and avocations will gain new meanings.

We ask, "What foundation may be established that we might build upon that will allow us to achieve these fantastic results? Where is it? What is it? How do we find it?"

The answer is not esoteric, and we do not have to travel far to find it. In fact, we may not have to travel at all. Where the answer lies is all around us and within us.

That sure, firm foundation is simply this: God is perfect love. His love circumscribes us and resides within us. We find this love by breaking down the walls of our preconceived notions and false ideals and allowing His love to flow in and ours to flow out. Launching from this premise, we will see how easily all our trials and tribulations fall into place.

Because God is perfect love, all that He allows us to experience, the seemingly bad, the hardships, the truly difficult and painful, as well as those things of pleasure and ease, must be for our benefit. The trials in life, if experienced with humility and with an understanding of God's ultimate purpose, teach us patience and foster our personal spiritual and emotional growth. Our being, that which makes us a complete person, can only be developed if there is some form of resistance.

To become physically strong, a movement is needed to overcome an opposing force. This builds muscle. To become spiritually and emotionally strong, we must move against an equivalent psychological barrier. These barriers are the tests and trials of life. They are gifts from God that allow us the necessary opportunities to strengthen our mental muscles and develop a Godlike character.

As we learn to view our life from Heavenly Father's point of view, we come to understand why He allows wars and contentions and some peoples and nations to feast while others starve in famine. We understand the loss of loved ones, even when those losses occur under the most unimaginable of circumstances. We understand why people act the way they do and why they are permitted to do so. We understand the confusion of politics and international policies. We understand our neighbors. We understand the confusions of personal existence. We have a clarity of life in general and in particular that we only dreamed possible but never really believed attainable.

Sadly, some people reject God because of this imperfect world. If we accept that God our Heavenly Father is perfect love, we will accept the perfection of this imperfect world and our imperfect lives.

Every sentient being at some point questions where he or she came from and where he or she is going. It is a curiosity that is endemic to the world's population. In asking that question, we begin to investigate realms outside our temporal existence and experience. When we explore these realms, we truly enter the world of the supernatural.

To alleviate the erroneous notion that the supernatural has nothing to do with Christian belief and theology, we should clarify what *supernatural* means and not what our imaginations or what unwitting teachings may conjure up in our minds. Sadly, people occasionally equate *supernatural* with the *occult*. This beautiful word has been perverted, as have so many others of late. A word properly used gives tremendous clarity to the meaning of the thought being expressed. So it is with *supernatural*. When we break the word into components, we have:

- *super*—meaning 1, over, above, on top of. 2, superior to
- *natural*—meaning 1, forming a part of, or arising from nature; in

accordance with what is found or expected in nature. 2, produced or existing in nature; real; not artificial or manufactured. (All definitions in this book come from *Webster's New World Dictionary of the American Language,* College Edition, copyright 1968.)

Supernatural is a word of exceeding clarity, importance, and meaning. With this in mind, we need to take extreme care to build our faith and belief upon that which is true, and although often difficult, we must cast aside false notions and ideas that are not grounded in fact. We should take comfort in clarity and simplicity and understand that supernatural is not mystical or magical and should not be tied to the occult. The supernatural is as real as the chair you are sitting on. It is also miraculous and divine.

Supernatural itself is defined as 1, existing or occurring outside the normal experience or knowledge of man; caused by other than the known forces of nature. 2, attributed to hypothetical forces beyond nature; miraculous; divine.

As stated in the first definition, the supernatural exists and it occurs. It is simply outside that which we normally experience. And, without a great measure of logical and reasonable rumination upon the subject, which most of us will admit to rarely have done, we cannot in reality know the supernatural. If, by chance, we have experienced an event we have termed supernatural, we generally chalk it up to being that which is completely beyond our capacity to understand and, at best, give the event a cursory examination rather than deeply pondering what and how it may have occurred. When an event is caused by other than known forces of nature, it does not invalidate the manifestation, rather it points to how severely limited our knowledge is of physics and the greater laws that govern the universe.

Addressing the second definition, if we attribute an event to a hypothetical force beyond our current understanding of nature or physics and then proceed to deny or invalidate the possibility of that event, we beg the question. In effect, we are saying this event could not occur because we don't know how it could occur and its occurrence doesn't follow the laws as we know them, so its occurrence is an impossibility.

However, our limited understanding of the governing laws of nature is no justification for denying realities. So these types of "unexplainable" events have been called miracles, divine acts, and unknowable. But, as we will see, miraculous acts of divinity simply follow the order of a higher set of governing principles and ordinances.

Isaiah tells us, "For my thoughts *are* not your thoughts, neither *are* your ways my ways, saith the Lord. For *as* the heavens are higher than the earth, so are my ways higher than your ways, and my thoughts than your thoughts" (Isaiah 55:8–9; emphasis added).

It is that which occurs *outside our normal experience* and *the miraculous and divine* that we will now examine. We will come to see that so many of the mysteries of the kingdom of God need not be mysteries at all. The following scriptures illustrate this philosophy:

> But there is a God in heaven that revealeth secrets, and maketh known to the king Nebuchadnezzar what shall be in the latter days. Thy dream, and the visions of thy head upon thy bed, are these. (Daniel 2:28)

> He answered and said unto them, Because it is given unto you to know the mysteries of the kingdom of heaven, but to them it is not given. (Matthew 13:11)

> Having made known unto us the mystery of his will, according to his good pleasure which he hath purposed in himself. (Ephesians 1:9)

> And for me, that utterance may be given unto me, that I may open my mouth boldly, to make known the mystery of the gospel. (Ephesians 6:19)

As we come to a more thorough understanding of words, terms, and the context within which facts, propositions, and premises are delineated, we begin to see and experience the simplicity and beauty of the scriptures and solve many of the "mysteries" of the kingdom. His divine plan for our eternal joy and happiness has been set forth plainly and succinctly in the Holy Scriptures so that we may be closer with Him in this life, as well as when our personal mortality ends.

How sad it is that so many teach that Heavenly Father is unknowable and that the scriptures are necessarily cryptic so that precious few may understand them. Throughout the ages, the masses have been wrongly taught that they must depend upon the multifarious interpretations of educated scholars. They have believed that only these scholars are possessed of the necessary education (by way of secular institutions) to interpret the scriptures and that only by this "learned wisdom" may man truly know God.

The written word of God has not always been available, and scriptures are often twisted, sometimes intentionally, with the result that people have been led away from the truth. Additionally, when the scriptures have been available, to circumvent the effort of searching the scriptures, people throughout the ages up to and including the present have asked for miracles to prove the existence of God and the truth of Christ's divinity. "Show me a miracle and I'll believe" is a common saying we hear too often from those who lack faith.

Regrettably, those poor souls who tempt the Lord with demands for proof have the concept backwards. Miracles are not for the convincing of people that God exists and Jesus is the Christ. If that were true, with all the miracles that have occurred and been documented from the time of Moses, through Christ's recorded mission and up to the present time, there should be no unbelievers. But the unbelievers abound. They fill our television programs and picture shows. They are in our schools and work places. They have inundated our legal system. They actively work to decimate our Constitution and the principles upon which this unique and great nation was founded. They are the lost and lonely among society.

The truth is that miracles rarely bring people to accept the divine and, as a consequence, rarely alter one's course of life for an extended period of time. The divine experience usually quickly fades as time and a lack of understanding erodes the experience.

A classic example is the documented exodus of Israel. Noted in Exodus 12:40–41, after more than four hundred years of bondage and servitude to Egypt, the population of the slave nation of Israel grew so great that Heavenly Father decreed the time had come to separate them from Pharaoh's rule and establish their sovereignty as a choice people. Numbers 1:45–46 sets the census of men age twenty and upward, who were capable of going to war, at over six hundred thousand. Add to that women, children, and elderly men, and this mass exodus was undertaken by at least one and a half million people.

At the beginning of their escape from Egyptian enslavement, the children of Israel were provided a miraculous manifestation of such magnitude that it would seemingly solidify that all their future acts would be consecrated to God. When en route to the promised land, with their escape blocked, it seemed certain that the Egyptian army would overtake them, resulting in a great loss of life. The Israelites were spared decimation by divine intervention.

To protect His chosen people, God commanded Moses, who was a prophet and the leader of the Israelite nation, "But lift thou up thy rod, and stretch out thine hand over the sea, and divide it: and the children of Israel shall go on dry ground through the midst of the sea" (Exodus 14:16).

That night the east wind blew continuously. When the time to depart arrived, the Red Sea parted to provide safe passage and access to a place of refuge and security from Pharaoh's pursuing army. After crossing on dry ground where "the waters were a wall unto them on their right hand, and on their left" (Exodus 14:22), the nation of Israel obtained safety on the far shore. With hard hearts and feverish zeal, their Egyptian foes were in the midst of crossing the parted sea in pursuit of the fleeing nation when, upon the further command of Moses, the waters then returned to their rightful place. The multitude that gave chase, including the Pharaoh's horses and his chariots, were killed. Israel witnessed the dead bodies of Pharaoh's soldiers strewn along the shore.

Additional miracles were provided. Free of their enemies, the Israelites traveled through the desert. As stores ran low, the people grew concerned. What would they eat? Where would they find the precious water needed in such an arid locale? Fearful and with increasing agitation, they confronted Moses. In answer to Moses' prayers, the mighty nation was provided manna from heaven. It appeared each morning, with the exception of the Sabbath day. For forty years, their needs were met. When the Israelites tired of this heaven sent sustenance, and desirous of meat, quail were provided for food. Under divine command, Moses struck a rock and water gushed forth to quench their thirst (see Exodus 17:5–6).

During the midst of this miraculous protection, Moses was directed to commune on the heights of a mountain with God for a period of forty days and nights. Acting under the direction of God, Moses brought down from the mount a set of divine instructions to be presented to this choice and favored people.

Moses descended from Mount Sinai expecting to join his people and present them with one of the greatest blessings they could receive. How heartbreaking it must have been upon his return from the mount and upon reuniting with his people to find this divinely protected nation worshipping a golden calf (see Exodus 32:1–5). It is hard for us to understand how quickly the people fell away from a belief in God with all that was presented to them. Yet regardless of the experienced miracles, that is exactly what happened.

The New Testament miracles performed by Jesus are legion. He turned water into wine. He healed the sick. He raised the dead. He made the blind to see. A touch on the hem of His garment and health was restored. He fed the multitude with a loaf of bread and a few fish.

He was crucified by unbelievers who had witnessed many of these events.

Miracles have rarely caused people to embrace a lasting belief in religious tenets or divinity. However, miracles often strengthen the faith and convictions of those who already believe. They are given to the faithful as a blessing and deliverance after all they could have done in a particular circumstance.

This leads to the first and foremost principle of the gospel: faith. If we are to believe in divinity, that belief will come through faith, not miracles.

Faith in the Lord Jesus Christ is the key that unlocks the door leading to exaltation. Faith is that intrinsic knowledge we possess, knowing that some event, thing, or occurrence is true and has, or will, come to pass even though we have no direct empirical evidence to substantiate our position or belief.

The Bible states, "Now faith is the substance of things hoped for, the evidence of things not seen" (Hebrews 11:1). Likewise, in the Book of Mormon, we read, "And now as I said concerning faith—faith is not to have a perfect knowledge of things; therefore if ye have faith ye hope for things which are not seen, which are true" (Alma 32:21).

The manifestation of that which has not been seen which is true comes about after we exercise our faith. The process of faith preceding knowledge of the miraculous and divine is exactly opposite to how we are taught to survive temporally. We learn in school to reason from fact to conclusion. This belief is so entrenched in secular thought and logic that the courts of our legal system echo with the objection, "Assuming facts not in evidence." Yet, that is exactly how we exercise faith. We assume the fact is true without any evidence. After that assumption, the Lord reveals the truthfulness of the fact in question and confirms the assumption/conclusion.

Some people are seemingly born with more or greater faith than others. For them, exercising faith requires little effort. Those who have not explored this realm naturally ask how they might obtain this gift.

Asking that question actually constitutes the first step, or the desire to have faith. If we have the desire for faith and to acknowledge the existence of

God the Father and His son, Jesus the Christ, we then must ask for that gift, believing our prayer will be answered. By that simple act, we have already exercised faith. God will then increase our faith if that is our desire.

How is faith increased? Through prayer and living a more Christ-like life. By becoming ever more humble and turning to God in all ways and in all circumstances. The more we exercise our faith, the more it is increased.

Faith Precedes the Miracle is a wonderful book by Spencer W. Kimball, the twelfth president of The Church of Jesus Christ of Latter-day Saints. The phrase taken from the title of his book has become a church standard.

Faith precedes the miracle. With and through faith, we can understand miracles for what they are. With faith, we see miraculous events that can go unnoticed by most. With faith, we attribute miracles to the proper authority. With faith, we realize that miracles are a gift to the penitent. With faith, we realize that miracles are manifestations of His divine love and a reward to the faithful. Through faith, as well as reasoning and revelation, we will establish the base and foundation from which our journey begins and ends. That base being His perfect love. It is upon this divine foundation of His perfect love that all else rests.

chapter two

HIS HOUSE OF ORDER

I often walk outside on a clear morning before the sunrise and experience awe and a calm peace at the wonders of the heavens. How beautiful are the creations of our God. How infinite in their scope and majesty. How comforting to know that in this society of man-made rush and confusion, we are surrounded by a cosmos of peace and order. In just those few morning minutes with nature, alone with the creations of our Heavenly Father, I am given a greater, clearer perspective of His great plan for our happiness and salvation.

You might suggest that the stars in the sky with their nuclear explosions, the violent reactions that form nebulae, the presence of comets and asteroids on a seemingly random path through space, and even the scientific evidence presented to support the "Big Bang" theory of the creation of the universe point to an infinite existence of chaos, chance, and random happenstance.

That suggestion would be wrong.

The layman needs to understand what the scientist knows. All actions of all the elements that compose the universe follow a defined set of predetermined laws. The scientific community is aware that they do not know those laws in their entirety. They find that things change. Some actions seem not to follow an established pattern. There are unexplained anomalies. To their credit, scientists incorporate corrections and clarifications to those laws they held to be true and have found to be, in fact, erroneous or inaccurate. Knowledge is built truth upon truth, line upon line, precept upon precept, and this they understand. Greater clarity gives greater understanding and prompts deeper questioning, which ultimately results in greater knowledge. And the circle begins again.

What the majority of scientists fail to perceive is that the laws of physics were instituted by God. Because God is the beginning and the end, His laws are eternal and unchanging. He applies those laws faultlessly.

God created the laws that govern the order of the universe, and as such, He cannot violate His own laws. Though the laws of the universe seem to change, they in fact do not. Science only discovers or clarifies deeper aspects of those laws. God's laws that govern the order of the universe pertain to multiple planes or dimensions as evidenced by the appearance of Christ to His apostles when they were meeting in a closed room, or when He was witnessed ascending out of sight of the mortals with whom He was conversing. Upon His resurrection, graves were opened, and bodies arose, went into the holy city, and appeared unto many (see Matthew 27:50–53). Christ walked on water and allowed Peter the same privilege (see Matthew 14:22–31).

The laws instituted by our Divine Creator encompass so much more than we are able to conceive that it is absurdly arrogant to think that He would arbitrarily change a law to fit a particular situation. As a perfect being, He does not institute imperfect plans. From the beginning, His universe, the heavens and the planets, were created to establish the perfect foundation for the existence of life. He does not capriciously change the laws that govern how worlds are formed, how stars are created, or how gravity functions.

It stands to reason that His house is a house of order. God would not want us to receive all knowledge and then negate His desire by allowing random, nonsensical events that make it impossible to learn that knowledge. As we have been commanded to reason individually and jointly with Him, reasoning must follow logical steps to a logical conclusion.

The purpose of logic is to determine correct from incorrect reasoning. A leads to B, and so forth. However, we must be careful to begin from not only a correct premise but a truthful one as well. If the premise from which we start is correct, then the conclusion will be also, regardless if the premise is true or not. A will lead to B with C being the logical conclusion. If the premise from which we start is true and correct, the conclusion will not only be correct but truthful as well. If argued that it is impossible to know the truth because truth must first be proved, then you have fallen into the secular trap of negating the efficacy of faith and, thus, revelation.

Faith is the first principle of the gospel, around which all truth will be revealed. Man's "discoveries" are simply revealed truths that come forth to further the will of divinity, and we will be blessed to receive those truths only when the timing is such to be in our best interest. Our best interest is God's best interest. Heavenly Father's perfection includes that of logic and order. His creations, therefore, must be those of an ordered universe. There are no random acts.

Scientists know some of His laws. Others they do not. But their pursuit for understanding continuously moves on. When scientists come to a sure knowledge of an event or premise, they have simply proved one of God's principles. If they will rely upon God and couple their knowledge and understanding with the spirit of enlightenment, it will be unfathomable the speed at which discoveries will occur. If they rely upon their own understanding, it will be like steering a ship without a rudder. They will occasionally bump into a truth and then flounder until the next chance meeting.

So it is with us in our pursuit to know of God's incredible plan. If we rely upon the understanding of man, we founder upon the rocks of confusion. Have you ever considered and been amazed at how many different religions and churches read the same scripture in the Bible and come up with such contrary and contradictory conclusions? Is this not in opposition to our Father's house of order? Would He give different sets of instructions for each different church and religion? Would He, in His perfect love, provide us with instructions for our salvation and then scramble those instructions to cause continuous conflict and confusion?

Of course not. Satan is the author of confusion and contention. The antithesis of chaos is order, and its author is God. The Perfect One wants us to enjoy clarity, peace, understanding, and a sure and true map to chart our lives. He wants us to know where we came from, why we are here, and where we are going. He has provided us with a straight and narrow path that leads to salvation. Straight and narrow so as to be the most direct route to heaven. He has given us signposts and guides, books and revelations. He answers our prayers. He would have us progress in an orderly fashion. He has given us His Son as a living example of what we are to do. And He *gave* His Son for all the things that we cannot do.

God's plan for our salvation is implemented line upon line and precept upon precept in three basic, distinct, and uniquely ordered phases. Because each phase involves where we lived, where we are living, or where we will live, they are called estates.

Jude, the brother of James and one of the brethren of Christ, penned a beautiful scripture in Jude 1:6: "And the angels which kept not their first estate, but left their own habitation, he hath reserved in everlasting chains under darkness unto the judgment of the great day."

This brief scripture contains marvelous information. The angels who failed to keep their first estate did so by choice. They were not forced to leave but did so of their own accord. They left their own habitation. They will be judged according to their choices.

Who were these angels? They were those spirit children of God who chose to follow Lucifer. Where was their habitation termed their first estate? It was in the presence of God the Father. We will look more closely in following chapters and find that the angels mentioned actually made up one-third of those who comprised the first estate. It is comforting to know that you and I and the rest of the inhabitants of this earth—past, present, and future—comprise the other two-thirds who kept their first estate.

Examining this short scripture establishes the fact that the first estate was a place of habitation. It was a place of life and living. It was an inhabited place where we dwelt along with innumerable others, including Christ and Lucifer. Our first estate was a place where we could exercise freedom of choice, or our moral agency. It was a place where issues were set forth upon which we could agree or disagree.

If it seems a little much to glean so many facts from such a small scripture, that is a point I can understand. However, this scripture, coupled with others, will be thoroughly examined and explained in subsequent chapters and will substantiate my claim. Our Heavenly Father would have us know the whole truth, and the above conclusions will not only be supported by many other scriptures but also, if we allow it, a personal testimony received from the Holy Ghost.

When we delve into and research the scriptures concerning our first estate, we find that it predates our earthly life. For convenience, we will refer to it as the premortal existence. The fact that we existed prior to mortality, the condition in which we find ourselves at the present time, infers we did not have physical, mortal bodies as we do now. Therefore, our bodies must have existed in a different state.

To establish the makeup of this realm, we need to set forth the basic tenets of the premortal existence, or our first estate. We are the actual children of God our Father. We were His spirit children prior to birth into mortality. We lived in His presence. We received instruction. We had freedom to exercise choice. And we grew and developed to a point that we needed a physical body for our further progression.

The fact that we do not remember this experience is critical to His plan. An all-knowing God has established two primary principles that are necessary for us to receive and exercise during mortality so that we may return to His presence. That we have forgotten our premortal existence and that we knew these facts is key to exercising the first principle of the gospel: faith.

Of course, what follows our first estate is our second estate—the second phase of His plan, or our mortal life. It is the temporal life we are now living. Of necessity, we came into this world to gain experiences. We are to be tried and tested, and a mortal, temporal, physical body is a necessary requirement for this. This fact is established at the beginning of the Bible and is repeated by theme and example throughout the scriptures. Adam and Eve were cast from the Garden of Eden to live by the sweat of their brow. They were to work and endure the vicissitudes of life, that those experiences would be for their benefit. The temptations of Christ, by Satan, are an example of what we are to expect in mortality. As recorded in Matthew 4:1–11, Jesus was led by the Spirit into the wilderness to undertake a forty-day fast. At the conclusion of His fast, at His weakest moment, He was besieged by the devil with all manner of temptations. Having rejected those temptations, Christ began His ministry.

As we read the New Testament, the Gospels recount the life of Jesus. He suffered privation, adversity, poverty, hardship, and temporal need. Christ Himself described succinctly His earthly life: "Foxes have holes, and birds of the air have nests; but the Son of man hath not where to lay his head" (Luke 9:58).

We need to experience pain and pleasure, heat and cold, joy and sorrows. We need to be dependent and have others depend upon us. We need to be part of a family. We need to accept responsibilities. We need to develop compassion and humility. We need to serve freely, without compunction or being compelled. We need to learn to love at all times and in all places. We need these and many other experiences, some of which can only be had by having a mortal body. And we need to have these experiences while being separated from the presence of our Heavenly Father.

Our third estate is our postmortal existence. It is when our temporal body has been laid to rest. It is the afterlife. It is all those events that take place after we die and our bodies are buried. It is a place of rest from the cares of this world. It is also a place of instruction, service, enlightenment, and choice. It is the place our spirits go to receive further instruction and await resurrection and the day of our judgment.

There is order to this existence. In fact, order is what changes existence into living. God is the creator. If there were no God, there would be no order, for order must hinge upon obedience to laws. He, or more properly, the laws He instituted are the glue that binds life, order, and the universe together. Science scratches the surface of this concept.

Scientists have found that things left to themselves fall into a state of disarray, confusion, and disorder. In science, this is called the second law of thermodynamics. This law states that the entropy (entropy measures the degree of disorder of a system) of an isolated system always increases and that when two systems are joined together, the entropy of the combined system is greater than the sum of the entropies of the individual systems.

If science proves that there is disorder in the universe, does not that invalidate God? The answer is no. The disorder that is recognized by the second law of thermodynamics is disorder on a micro scale. When contrasted to the universe as a whole, there will be an order to what seems to be hapless circumstance.

A simple example on a practical level is a lawless society, or a society in which laws are selectively obeyed. When people choose not to obey laws, chaos ensues and society collapses. When laws are obeyed, society functions in an orderly manner. However, viewed from a larger, or macro perspective, the universe continues to function in an orderly and uninter-rupted manner regardless of what is taking place "below." God instituted the laws that govern the universe. Order comes from organization. Our temporal lives are ordered and patterned after the life we lived in our first estate.

True, when we examine the wayward condition of the world in general and individuals in particular, we may argue against this life being patterned after our heavenly abode. But such is not the case. We must realize that Satan has been given great reign in affecting worldly events. His influence reaches far and wide. And his influence is necessary to provide the opposition we need so that we may chose right from wrong. No, this world in the beginning was patterned after the world from which we came. It is the way it is now because of man's exercise of free will.

Heavenly Father's house, or all that He possesses, including this little planet we call earth, is a house of order. He established order in our first estate, and beginning with Adam and Eve, He established order for our second estate. However, as we are still children in relation to eternal growth and progression, we have made a mess of "His" house.

If we understand that He will have perfect order once again in our third estate, or postmortal life, we would be wise to continually monitor our progress and obedience during our present estate.

It is statement of fact, warning, admonition, exhortation, and encouragement that no unclean thing can enter the kingdom of heaven. Let us understand this most salient point: to be clean means more than to just be baptized; we must also be orderly. To be clean, we must follow the orders of our Lord and Master. To be clean, we must grow or obtain wisdom in an orderly fashion, line upon line, precept upon precept. To be clean, we must repent and be forgiven. To be clean, we must follow the commandments.

God has shown us how to be clean. He has shown us how to be orderly. He has promised us that by being clean, we may enter the kingdom of heaven. He has shown us what cleanliness is.

Lucifer was not clean nor was he ordered. He would have instituted chaos and contention in heaven as he now has on earth. He was cast out of heaven along with his followers, he to become Satan and they to become the sons of perdition (see Revelation 12:9).

It is true more so than we can imagine that cleanliness is next to Godliness. It would do us well to remember that God resides in heaven. If we want to reside and be next to God, we must be clean, and we must be orderly to live in His house of order.

chapter three

HIS PERFECT LOVE

Our Heavenly Father's attributes are many, and they are perfect. He is all-knowing, all-powerful, all-caring, and the embodiment of perfection. He is perfect peace, and He is perfect joy. And, underscoring these and all other characteristics, He possesses the sure foundation upon which all His wishes and desires for us are based: perfect love.

Because God is perfect in all ways, we can correctly infer many aspects of His personality, desires, and will. I cannot imagine a being of perfect love that would not want us, His children, to know of Him or to know of His desires, wants, wishes, and plans for us. To what purpose would it serve to keep those things secret?

If we understand His perfect love in all aspects of our lives and apply that understanding at all times and in all places, we will experience a continually deepening knowledge of the mysteries of His kingdom. Our Heavenly Father wishes to bless us as richly as He can. It is up to us to realize that if we want blessings, we must put ourselves in a position to be blessed. We are the limiting factor, not God. In His infinite wisdom, He will open our eyes and minds to as much knowledge, understanding, and enlightenment as He is able. He will never give us more or allow us to be tempted with more than we are can responsibly bear. Our responsibility is to always remember that to whom much is given, much is required (Luke 12:48).

His perfect love is what allows us, if we choose, to find joy and understanding in all the events that make up the fabric of our lives. Whether our lives are relatively free from the rents and tears of tribulation or if they are a patchwork quilt of sorrows and trials, we can find peace and joy in knowing who God our Father is and His desire for us. While it is true that certain events take more time to come to terms with than others, that is the essence of growth. In *De Providentia,* Lucius Annaeus Seneca wrote, "Calamity is virtue's opportunity." We must all learn this lesson, regardless of era or position. We simply need to see events from God's perspective and not ours.

Many think our Heavenly Father is unknowable. Others believe He is an essence filling the universe. Some feel He manipulates our lives and the events that shape them. Still others feel we are pawns for His amusement. Many believe our lives are predestined, and it doesn't matter what we do.

All of these individuals are wrong, and it is tragic that these erroneous concepts are perpetuated from generation to generation.

For a moment, in your mind, set aside the family conflicts you may be enduring and reflect on the love you have for your family. Reflect on what your children mean to you. Think of your spouse and the love that comes forth in sweet peace and joy from your blessed union. Close your eyes and feel the pure and pristine love you have for your sons and daughters. The pure love we feel for our children is the closest we can come to the feelings of pure love God has for humanity. Now imagine experiencing that love to the greatest depths of your ability. At a point beyond that is where the pure love of God begins. And it grows from there.

Do you want your children to grow up to be as happy as they can be? Do you want them to be better than you are? Do you want more for them than you have obtained in all aspects of your life? Do you wish them to become greater than you are, both temporally and spiritually? Do you wish them to have greater peace, joy, and love in their lives than you have? If the answer to any of the questions is yes, you have a minuscule understanding of our Heavenly Father's love for us. This is why we have been given families.

Our Heavenly Father's love for us is personal and special. You and I are equally as important to God as anybody else. Jeremiah 31:3 states that "the Lord hath appeared of old unto me, saying, Yea, I have loved thee with an everlasting love: therefore with loving kindness have I drawn thee."

John 16:27 records that "for the Father himself loveth you, because ye have loved me, and have believed that I came out from God."

And finally, in John 17:23, "I in them, and thou in me, that they may be made perfect in one; and that the world may know that thou hast sent me, and hast loved them, as thou hast loved me."

For God to want anything less for us than that which He possesses would be a flaw in His character. Because He is a perfect being, this would be impossible.

We must remember that all He does and all He allows to happen are ultimately for our benefit and the benefit of all humanity. The deeper our spirituality, the greater our understanding of this concept. His perfect love demands it must be so.

The purpose of any parent is to rear children in love and safety and to provide them opportunities to gain experience and to learn and grow to their greatest potential. A parent's objective is also to instill in children virtues, values, respect, and the desire to aid their fellow man; to be there in times of sadness, trials, and temptations; to share joy; to teach children the correct use of moral agency; to allow children to make mistakes when they exercise their agency incorrectly; to help them learn from those mistakes; to love their children unconditionally; and to lead and guide our children for as long as we, their parents, live. If we have done our job quite well, our influence upon our children does not end with our passing, rather it will serve as a guide throughout their lives.

How great must be His divine desires for us? If we want our children to surpass us in all the positive aspects of our lives, what would God want for us? We know that God is perfect. We know that we cannot exceed perfection. However, it is possible for us to rise to perfection. We all know that there is and will be only one perfect person who has walked the face of this earth, and that is Jesus Christ. No matter how we try, we will not reach perfection in mortality. However, because of our inability to reach perfection in this life, Our Heavenly Father has given us the greatest gift He could—His Son, Our Lord and Savior Jesus Christ and the gift of His Atonement. "For God so loved the world, that he gave his only begotten Son, that whosoever believeth in him should not perish, but have everlasting life" (John 3:16). Because of His perfect love for us, He allowed the sacrifice of His son. No one has loved us that much. No one could love us more.

OTHER THOUGHTS
AND REVIEW

I remember building a model airplane with my father. I was a young boy, and like most boys my age, I was fascinated with the prospects of actually making something fly. I had graduated from simple plastic replicas of the World War II flying machines to the lofty realm of working models.

My first flying plane was of the kit variety. I believe the model was called the Ranger 27. It consisted of a balsa wood frame of sticks, which formed a square fuselage. The wing sat atop the body. It resembled the Piper Cub airplanes of today, although it was proportionally longer in the body, and no plane, be it a model or an actual machine, could match its exquisite beauty and style.

My father and I spent hours gluing the wood frame together, covering the skeleton of the plane with the red tissue paper skin, and finally, applying just the right amount of liquid dope to the skin to tighten it and give it strength. The model was powered by a rubber band-driven propeller and had a fixed spring wire and wheel landing gear.

The Ranger's maiden flight took place in a beautiful grassy field in Griffith Park. We wound the propeller over and over until the rubber band was twisted in knots. With great excitement and a little anxiety, my father launched the plane.

More to our amazement than I care to admit, that beautiful plane soared red and majestic through the afternoon sky. It took off quickly and climbed to a low altitude, its propeller biting into the air. And when the power had dispersed from its driver, it continued to float in an effortless grace that seemed to make it a part of the wind and sky. It was where it belonged.

There were many parts, steps, and instructions that I needed to follow to be successful in my endeavor. Any mistake at any phase of my attempt would have kept me from accomplishing my goal. For the Ranger to fly, it had to be perfect. Yet to achieve that perfection was beyond my ability. I was not capable of doing it myself, but I had my father there to guide me. I was given both written and spoken instructions. I had an example to follow. I had someone to lead and encourage me. And when my ability and efforts were not equal to the task, my father was there to do for me what I could not do myself.

Our Heavenly Father's plan is a lot like building that plane. To reach perfection, we are given instructions, steps to follow, guides to help us along the way, and someone to do for us those things we cannot do for ourselves.

After a lifetime of questioning and searching for enlightenment and truth, and to then integrate those truths into a cohesive whole, I have discovered, along with millions of others, the key elements that have made that integration possible. Whenever I am tossed by the storms of life and the confusions of the world roil the waters of my mind, I return to the safe harbor. It is a harbor of peace and tranquility. It is a harbor of light and understanding. It is a harbor of truth and righteousness. It is a harbor of learning and growth. It is the harbor for understanding the mysteries of life and the kingdom of God.

But to enter the harbor there is always a price to be paid, a toll of sorts. It is not a price that depletes my resources, nor that of any who choose to enter, for the harbor is open to all. It is infinite in size and scope and can accommodate all explorers who have ever existed, who exist at this moment, or who will come to pass. The harbor is perfect because it was created by the Perfect One, but there is a price to be paid.

Faith. This is the price, a price that costs us nothing yet promises everything. The process is counterintuitive. Usually we must receive something before being able to spend. Here we spend first. We spend what we already have, and when we spend it, we receive more than what we had to begin with. It is never depleted, and the more faith is spent, the more it grows.

For those who have not exercised their faith, the promised reward seems almost unimaginable: eternal life and exaltation; peace and joy; love and harmony.

When you exercise faith, you find that straight and narrow path our Heavenly Father has created for us that leads us back to His presence. Along that path are signposts, guides, and instructions. You will find they come in many forms. The more you spend your faith, the clearer those helps and instructions will become. The greater your willingness to accept and follow those instructions, the greater your understanding and enlightenment becomes. And that leads to an increase in faith. That beautiful circle of faith and understanding grows like the circles made by a pebble tossed into a pond, ever expanding in truth and knowledge, and ever-increasing in scope for love and compassion.

I cannot emphasize it enough. God is love. God is perfection. Everything He does and allows to happen is for our own best interest and that of humanity. God wants us to be as perfect as He is and to have all that He has. He will not let us travel the path back home alone. And He has not kept His instructions secret. He has given us His plan for our happiness and salvation, and it is based upon His house of order and His perfect love.

SECTION II:
THE PURPOSE OF HIS PLAN: TO BE AS HE IS

chapter five

TO RETURN
TO HIS PRESENCE

Many years have passed since that defining experience of my youth, which I described in the first chapter of this book. During most of those years I struggled, as do all that have grown to maturity, with the myriad trials of temporal existence. Teenage years were filled with insecurity and the need for social acceptance. Vietnam, like the sword of Damocles, hung over the heads of all young men who were of the proper age and health to serve their country. When I was drafted to fight in that war, it seemed as if the hair that held the sword was quickly beginning to fray.

My parents and I said our farewells in autumn 1970. Standing on the sidewalk outside of the Los Angeles Induction Center for the Armed Services, we embraced and shared our loving good-byes. The aching fear of the dismal prospects that the future most assuredly held went unspoken. Deep in our hearts, we were terrified that our farewells would be the last we ever shared.

A miracle in my life was about to unfold. I did not fight in that war.

I received my training at Fort Lewis, Washington. By a power and grace that I came to fully understand years later, my company was sent to Germany to serve our tour of duty. Two weeks prior to the date we were to receive our traveling orders, and we were called to stand a company formation. We were addressed by the battalion commander, who spoke directly and to the point. He spoke concerning all the men who had been trained at this facility from the beginning of the war to the present. And he spoke particularly concerning us.

"You all have orders for Vietnam," he said. "For the first time, at Fort Lewis, in the history of this war, an entire company's orders have been changed. With the exception of those of you who are going to N.C.O. Academy, and those of you who are going to Airborne, the rest of you will be going to Germany."

Though this was a most fortuitous event and was hailed with exuberant cheers and exhilaration by nearly all of the company, I experienced a shocking depression. I was drafted to serve a two-year commitment. I left college, girlfriend, home, and family for the obvious task of fighting overseas. To cope with my newfound circumstances and to calm the fears of what could possibly happen to me, I adopted the attitude that I most likely would be killed. Facing up to and accepting the most horrific of possible outcomes for my situation gave me peace and serenity. To be prepared for the worst event that may occur allowed me to live fully in the present and embrace my supposed probability.

I had rationalized the need for being drafted. My depression at the change of orders was due to having my house of rationalization razed to the ground. I could not make any sense of my present situation, and it seemed to have absolutely no purpose.

Although I decided to make the best of my most fortunate situation, I found the boredom and monotony of being a "pretend" soldier during a time of war to be at odds with my personality and temperament. To not stand alongside those of my country and help with the fight that continued to wage seemed to be not only wrong but also contradictory to the entire purpose of being drafted. Let me fight or let me out.

Fighting was not to be the case. My attempt to submit a request to transfer to Vietnam was denied. No such requests would be honored. It was early spring of 1971, and our involvement in the war was starting to wind down.

I served my time in the service to the best of my ability. I had many wonderful experiences in Europe, and made German, French, Spanish, and Swiss friends. I realized I was a guest in these countries and conducted myself accordingly. I was treated as a king. And when my tour of duty was over, I received an honorable discharge in April of 1972.

There is a culture shock we experience after living in a foreign land for an extended period of time and then returning home. Although I was welcomed and received most graciously by my European hosts and I felt completely at ease and confident, I was still in an unfamiliar environment. Though I was filled with the joy and exuberance of independence and freedom, there existed within me a need for comfort that only familiar surroundings and family can fill.

How joyous it was to return home! How comforting to have the warmth and safety that only a family can provide! Free from the uncertainties of fate and the fetters of unsolicited servitude, I was finally back where I came from. I was back where I belong.

The joy and happiness my parents felt upon my safe return was tremendous. The joy and happiness I experienced was humbling.

During my separation from my family, I came to know of our deep love for each other in a way that only separation can bring. It was a revelatory time that allowed me to realize and appreciate on a much grander scale the selfless love my parents had given me through so many years. Coupled with this feeling of gratitude and humility was a feeling of sorrow, sorrow for things I did and things I did not do. I gave my best effort to repay them for all the love and effort they put forth on my behalf. Sadly, I fell far short in my attempts at restitution. I was never able to come close, let alone fully repay all they had done for me. I was still maturing, and I was still making mistakes.

Did I disappoint my parents? Most certainly. Did I make poor choices? Yes. Did their love for me ever fail? No. I was always welcomed with open arms.

My parents were an example of pure parental love. My mistakes were not ignored, but neither was I condemned. I was loved to the best of their ability, for as long as they lived.

How deeply they longed for my return. How deep was their joy when I did return. Their one and only and greatest desire was for my safe return home, that I might live with them again. And, as much as my independent and prideful soul tried to deny it, that was truly my greatest desire also.

I understand the pure love my parents had for me. Having children of my own has allowed me to experience this indescribable feeling for myself. But I am mortal. I am imperfect. I am flawed in character and actions. Although I put forth my greatest effort to conduct myself as a gentleman and embody the example of Christ our Savior, I fall woefully short. The magnitude of Christ's love, and that of His father, reaches far beyond my comprehension. What I do know is that God's love is given and expressed in ways and in depths that my imperfect love cannot parallel. My love knows time. His is eternal. My love has limits. His is endless.

When I reflect on how badly my parents longed for my safe return home, I think how much more so must my Father in heaven long for my return.

chapter six

PERSPECTIVE AND INSTRUCTIONS

The first several years of a child's life is filled with wondrous adventure. Sights and sounds are discovered. Fingers and toes are delightful playthings. Awareness of a body develops. Imitated noises become a vocabulary. Full-fledged mobility is achieved. You teach your children manners and proper behavior. They learn how to share. They experience a wonderful phase of emotional, physical, and intellectual growth.

At the proper time, based upon their general development, they are ready for a new experience. They will enter a place of higher learning that challenges and tests their emotional, intellectual, and physical skills. They begin elementary school.

When they start school, your children are separated from you for hours. They don't have you there to answer their questions and to lead, guide, instruct, and comfort them. You have taught your children that other people can instruct them, and they must listen to and obey those individuals. You have given your authority to people you trust who will stand in your stead, as your proxy, until your children return home.

While your children are gone, you will have concerns, worries, and sometimes tears. Would you send your children away from you without proper preparation? Of course not.

Because of your love for them, you gave your children instructions on how to behave, what to do and not to do. You gave them instructions concerning their education, behavior, and safety. You want your children's education to equal or surpass your education. You hope for their happiness. You wish for them positive experiences. And most of all, your wish above all other wishes that they will return home safely.

Would a loving Heavenly Father, who is perfect in love and compassion, want anything less for His children? Would He allow us to go away from Him without the proper preparation and instructions? Would He allow us to descend to this world of trials, tests, and dangers without having someone here whom He trusts with His authority to lead and instruct us? Would He send us here and allow us to wander aimlessly trying to find our way back home to Him?

He would not.

God has given us instructions. They have come in the form of commandments, more than the ten that are so little read and less often followed. They also come in the form of revelations, both personal and general. God has given us prayer that we may inquire and receive direction. He has given us people ordained with His divine authority to lead and guide us, people who may speak on His behalf. These people are His prophets. The holy scriptures are laced with instructions that delineate correct and proper spiritual and temporal behavior and what we must do to return to His presence.

We are to search the scriptures, pray, and ponder. Then we use the power of reason God has given us. Additionally, we may receive the gift of discernment to determine correct from incorrect teachings, reasoning, and practices.

Our Heavenly Father wants to hide nothing from us. He gave His Only Begotten Son to stand as a witness and to provide us proper instructions concerning His plan. He wants us to know His will.

Because He is perfect love, His wish is that we may live with Him again.

chapter seven

THE GODHEAD

Absolutely essential in our quest is a clear understanding of the Godhead. This term, though not found in the Bible, depicts the unity in word, deed, power, and authority of God, our Heavenly Father; His son, Jesus Christ; and the Holy Ghost. These three beings constitute the Godhead. I testify that they are three distinct personages. They are as distinct from each other as you are from your neighbors.

Before undertaking any project, we must know what tools to use and the purpose of each tool. It is no different for us in our endeavor to understand God's plan for our salvation. We must know the purpose of God, Jesus Christ, and the Holy Ghost. Though they are one in purpose, they are distinct in personage. Each plays an individual role in the plan and serves us as individual tools. Their goal is the same. Their duties are different.

The first member of the Godhead is Heavenly Father. Our Heavenly Father's purpose concerning His children is the same purpose as we have in relation to our sons and daughters. Fortunately for us, He possesses two wonderful advantages. His love is perfect, and He is eternal. His instructions and guidance are not constrained by time and mortality, age or infirmity. He is the same today as He was yesterday and will be tomorrow (see Revelation 1:8). In Malachi 3:6, we read, "For I am the Lord, I change not." And in Hebrews 13:8, "Jesus Christ the same yesterday, and to day, and for ever." God makes no mistakes. His purpose concerning the Godhead is to stand as the ultimate leader and guide.

The second member of the Godhead is Jehovah, or Jesus Christ. Given to us so we might learn from His example, His crowning duty and glory were achieved by His atoning sacrifice. Are not the greatest leaders and teachers those who lead and teach by how they live their lives? It must be so, for God gave His Only Begotten Son to be the perfect example for mankind. Christ's life eclipses all others in adhering to the commandments and conveying His Father's will. The greatest gift we can receive is His Son, Jesus Christ. He was given to us not only to make an atonement for our sins, something we cannot do, but also to be the example of all that we must do to receive the greatest blessings from God.

He is the example of righteousness. He is the first fruits of all our Father's immortal and exalted children. In John 14:6, Christ shows us the way and that He is "the way, the truth and the life: no man cometh unto the Father, but by me." That is no idle scripture. He is perfect as His Father in heaven is perfect. He came to earth to lead, guide, and teach us. He came to be our example. He has given us temporal and spiritual laws. He ordained prophets and apostles to carry on His work. He taught his disciples. He showed us his Father's plan. He taught us all the neces-sary principles and ordinances for eternal life and exaltation. Because we are incapable of achieving perfection in this mortal life, Christ took upon Him our sins that through His grace we may be forgiven by our Father. He has shown us everything we must do to return to our Father's presence. He is the mediator between God and us.

May we not substitute God and Jesus in all things? Under the direction of God the Father, Jesus formed the worlds. Christ's actions are those of His Father. To be sinless and about His Father's business (see Luke 2:49) is testi-mony to that fact. A reading of Hebrews 1:1–4, 6, 8–10 provides wonderful insight and clarity into the nature of God the Father and Jesus Christ.

> God, who at sundry times and in divers manners spake in time past unto the fathers by the prophets, hath in these last days spoken unto us by *his* Son, whom he hath appointed heir of all things, by whom also he [Jesus Christ] made the worlds; who being the brightness of *his* [God; Heavenly Father] glory, and the express image of his person, and upholding all things by the word of his power, when he [Jesus Christ] had by himself purged our sins, sat down on the right hand of the Majesty on high; and again, when he [God; Heavenly Father] bringeth in the firstbegotten into the world, he saith, and let all the angels of God worship him [Jesus Christ].
>
> But unto the Son [Jesus Christ] *he* [God; Heavenly Father] *saith,* Thy throne, O God, *is* for ever and ever: a sceptre of righteousness *is* the sceptre of thy kingdom. [God the Father is calling Christ, God.] Thou hast loved righteousness, and hated iniquity; therefore God [Heavenly Father], *even* thy God, hath *anointed thee with the oil* of gladness above thy fellows. And,

Thou, Lord [Jesus Christ], in the beginning hast laid the foundation of the earth; and the heavens are the works of thine hands.
(emphasis added)

A complete work comprising many volumes could be written on
the epistle to the Hebrews. However, examining just some of what is
contained in the above verses will hopefully bring us some measure of
enlightenment. Here we find fantastic information. God spoke to our
fathers of old through the prophets. He speaks today to us through their
prophecies. Christ spoke and instructed the apostles. Christ is the heir of
all things. Christ made the worlds, our earth, and the heavens. Christ is
the brightness, glory, and the express image of God the Father. Christ will
receive a throne and a kingdom.

In verse 8, we are given an absolutely clear declaration that Christ is
a God. Heavenly Father calls Jesus Christ God! Here is a statement that
gives definitive proof that there is a plurality of Gods. The establishment
of this fact is particularly significant in light of Christ's pronouncement of
this fact to the Pharisees that would then serve to hasten His crucifixion.

In verse 9, we are also instructed in one of the sacred ordinances instituted prior to the creation of this earth and the heavens. The ordinance
is that of being set apart to follow a specific course of action. That this
ordinance was performed in the premortal existence is evidenced by the
fact that Christ was set apart by God the Father, Himself. He was set apart
from His fellow brethren to perform certain acts. He was authorized by one
having authority to establish and carry out certain function and duties.

Under the auspices of His Father, He was authorized, through that
blessing, to perform specified duties in the premortal world, as well as
during His earthly sojourn. We have established, as fact, by the exemplar
Jesus Christ, foreordination. As our leader in the premortal realm, as well
as on earth, Christ was the first to receive what would become a necessary
component of carrying out God's plan of salvation. We must conclude,
then, that we, also, have received the blessings of foreordination, if we are
to follow Christ and be as our Father is. The salient factor is, of course,
that foreordination is only efficacious if exercised through agency. This is
what separates foreordination from predestination. God would have us
choose of our own free will.

Lastly, a personage of spirit and not yet possessing a mortal body is the
Holy Ghost, the third member of the Godhead. He is also known as the
Holy Spirit and the Holy Spirit of Truth, the Testator, and the Holy Spirit

of Promise. His purpose and mission is to be our comforter and to bear witness to us of the truth. He is there to help us in choosing right from wrong. He helps us determine correct from incorrect reasoning. He is the means by which we communicate with God, in the name of Christ. It is of paramount importance that we recognize the prompting of the Holy Ghost, for by the Holy Ghost we receive God's answers to our prayers.

We all have had moments in our lives when we have felt prompted to do or not to do something. We occasionally experience "intuitive" knowledge relating to some situation or other. There are times when we know something is intrinsically correct or true. This is the prompting of the Holy Spirit. The Holy Ghost communicates with our spirit in a way we do not understand but recognize by a mental and physical manifestation. That does not lessen the truthfulness of our experience. The more we listen and attune ourselves to the promptings of the Holy Spirit, the easier those promptings are recognized.

Many people describe the manifestation of this experience as a still, small voice. For others, it is a warm feeling. For some, it is a feeling of calm and peace. Still others experience a tingling within their breast. Whatever form it takes, we must learn to recognize those manifestations and promptings.

Look back in your life to some event when you experienced pure innate or natural knowledge accompanied by one of those feelings. That was a prompting of the Holy Ghost. When you learn to recognize that prompting and live in accordance with all promptings from the Holy Ghost, along with obeying the commandments, you may ultimately know the truth of all things.

There is one thing of which to be absolutely certain: the communication to us by the Holy Spirit is always calm, peaceful, and sure and is experienced on a core level. It is never experienced as wild excitement or exuberance. We may become excited and enthusiastic after receiving a prompting under certain given circumstances, and that would be a normal reaction, especially if the prompting leads to good news or joy. But the prompting itself is never one of overt excitement. The Holy Ghost is the Comforter. He is calm and assured. He is peaceful. He is perfect grace and love just as is our Heavenly Father and Jesus Christ.

As you read this book, let your heart be open to the promptings of the Holy Spirit, the feeling within your body that speaks of validity and the correctness of the gospel principles being discussed or revealed. When you do, you will recognize that God is speaking directly to you by that

Spirit. Let the Holy Spirit speak to your spirit.

For those seeking the truth, James, the brother of Jesus, wrote in James 1:5–6: "If any of you lack wisdom, let him ask of God, that giveth to all men liberally, and upbraideth not; and it shall be given him. But let him ask in faith, nothing wavering. For he that wavereth is like a wave of the sea driven with the wind and tossed."

When we have studied a situation and pondered and prayed about it, Heavenly Father will manifest the answer to our prayer by the power of the Holy Spirit of Truth. That Spirit will let us know the veracity of our conclusion. We need to be humble and as little children and accept the answer we are given, even if that answer is not the one we were hoping for.

Though they are three distinct individuals and personalities, and though their duties and missions are different, the Godhead shares one common goal for mankind. Together, these three members of the Godhead unite to provide us a way to communicate with Heavenly Father. Through them, we are given information, direction, discernment, knowledge, revelation, comfort, peace, and all things necessary for our growth and success. When we are unable to do for ourselves, they carry us. Combined, they are a unit pledged to carry out the plans of Him who stands at their head.

Their organization is brilliant. Heavenly Father, with infinite wisdom, establishes a plan for the salvation of all who will listen and obey. His Son, who must pass through mortality, shows us through the manner in which He lived His life and by what He taught, what we must do to return to dwell with our Father. Knowing that it is impossible for us to be sinless, the Godhead is united in understanding and agreement that the Father will sacrifice His Son, the Son will sacrifice His life to do for us what we cannot do for ourselves, and the Holy Ghost will testify of the truthfulness of it all.

Upon the successful implementation of that aspect of Heavenly Father's plan, the Holy Ghost acts as the facilitator for communication, comfort, and truth. Christ promised His apostles He would not leave them comfortless (see John 15:26). Another comforter was promised them. And the Holy Ghost fulfills that promise to this day, comforting not only His apostles but His disciples as well. He leads, guides, instructs, and comforts all who heed God's plan.

Because God is not the author of confusion, He gave us the Holy Ghost along with the aforementioned recipe for finding the truth.

SECTION III:

THE PREMORTAL EXISTENCE

chapter eight

WHERE DOES LIFE BEGIN,
AND WHERE DO WE COME FROM?

Our universe and all that is in it was created by the organization of matter. Matter is matter and always will be. That matter can change form is a certainty due to the fact that matter is composed of elements. The notion or idea that some matter, element, or medium comes from nothing is a false premise. Joseph Smith stated this fact in April 1844, and it is recorded in *The Teachings of the Prophet Joseph Smith* (see 301–2, 350–52). This concept is a founding principle of modern science; however, it was not universally adopted until well after the declaration by the Prophet Joseph (see footnotes for above pages in *Teachings*).

God obeys the laws He created, and He organized the elements to suit His purposes based upon those laws. Were not the earthly bodies of Adam and Eve organized from the dust (elements) of the earth? We are assured so in Genesis. And did not God breathe the breath of life into Adam and, by inference, Eve? He most certainly did. This life that was "breathed" into them was their spirit. The uniting of their physical body and their spirit caused each of them to become a living soul. This is clearly stated in Genesis 2:7 and 1 Corinthians 15:44–45.

As we begin to examine our lives, we invariably ask the questions: Where does life begin and where do we come from? The usual answer in secular circles is that life begins somewhere between conception and birth. But doesn't our spirit live? When did our spirit come into being and where? And what exactly is our spirit?

The answer, like most of those with which we are concerned, is not that complicated. A perusal of the scriptures provides a clear understanding of these elemental but profoundly important questions.

Our spirit began sometime between our spirit conception and our spirit birth, eons prior to our mortal existence. It began when we became the spirit offspring of our Heavenly Father. We are actually, literally, and truly His spirit children.

Where we came from is where we lived before our mortal birth. We existed as spirits and lived with our Heavenly Father as surely as did Jesus Christ. The fact that we are the children of God also clarifies why we are all brothers and sisters.

Our spirit is the abode of our intelligence. It embodies our thoughts and feelings. It facilitates the part of us that reasons and gains knowledge. We must use extreme caution to not confuse our spirit body with our intelligence. While in mortality, we commonly think of our spirit as the thinking entity of our physical tabernacle. In fact, our spirit, or spirit body, houses our intelligence, much like our earthly body houses our spirit body (*Teachings,* 353).

Our spirit is composed of highly refined material (*Teachings,* 301–2). It allows us ethereal locomotion. Put quite simply, our spirit is our primary "body." Our spirits are physical, although in a much more pure and refined state than our mortal bodies. As a substance becomes refined, its more gross elements are discarded, and what material is left resonates at a higher frequency. It functions in a state of higher, or greater, energy. The molecular, atomic, and subatomic elements vibrate with a higher frequency. So it is with our spirit. Remembering that Christ was given to us as the perfect example, let us see what was exemplified regarding our spirit existence.

As a preface, we must understand that the effect upon us of seeing God the Father or His Son Jesus Christ is one and the same. They are alike in mind, manner, power, and glory. Radiance is an aspect of the glory of God and Christ that the natural man cannot withstand. With the effect being the same whether we see the first or second member of the Godhead, what subsequently transpires becomes clear. It matters not whether the Lord referred to and seen is Heavenly Father or Jesus Christ.

The Lord in the Old Testament usually referred to is Jesus Christ, also known as Jehovah. And in Isaiah 6:1, we read, "In the year that king Uzziah died I saw also the Lord sitting upon a throne, high and lifted up, and his train filled the temple."

I have heard more times than I care to remember the statement that no man can see the Lord and live. This belief emanates, I feel, from a lack of understanding of the scripture in Exodus 33:20 and a failure to read any further. "And he said, Thou canst not see my face: for there shall no man see me, and live."

This seems to be a direct contradiction to the statement given only nine verses prior in Exodus 33:11: "And the Lord spake unto Moses face to face, as a man speaketh unto his friend."

If God is the author of order and truth, how is this conflict resolved?

We must refer back to what was previously stated and exercise the premise that God is perfect in all ways, and through His perfect love, He will manifest the truth unto us. We know He can do all things. He can reveal himself, and He can conceal himself. He can protect, and He can destroy.

The resolution to these seemingly contradictory statements is actually quite simple. When Moses saw God face to face, Moses was "in the spirit," meaning that he was under the divine protection of God. He was transfigured. As a result of that transfiguration, note what transpired between Moses and the children of Israel in Exodus 34:28–35:

> And he was there with the Lord forty days and forty nights; he did neither eat bread, nor drink water. And he wrote upon the tables the words of the covenant, the Ten Commandments. And it came to pass, when Moses came down from mount Sinai with the two tables of testimony in Moses' hand, when he came down from the mount, that Moses wist not that the skin of his face shone while he talked with him.
>
> And when Aaron and all the children of Israel saw Moses, behold, the skin of his face shone; and they were afraid to come nigh him. And Moses called unto them; and Aaron and all the rulers of the congregation returned unto him: and Moses talked with them. And afterward all the children of Israel came nigh: and he gave them in commandment all that the Lord had spoken with him in mount Sinai.
>
> And till Moses had done speaking with them, he put a vail on his face. But when Moses went in before the Lord to speak with him, he took the vail off, until he came out. And he came out, and spake unto the children of Israel that which he was commanded. And the children of Israel saw the face of Moses, that the skin of Moses' face shone: and Moses put the vail upon his face again, until he went in to speak with him.

The statement that no *man* can see God and live is true pertaining to the *natural man.* The natural man is the state that we find ourselves in at the present time without God's protection. A natural man cannot withstand the full glory of God. It is too intense, brilliant and penetrating. However, look at what clarity we receive concerning the apparent contradiction when we read Exodus 33:21–23:

"And the Lord said, Behold, there is a place by me, and thou shalt stand upon a rock: And it shall come to pass, while my glory passeth by, that I will put thee in a clift of the rock, and will cover thee with my hand while I pass by: And I will take away mine hand, and thou shalt see my back parts: but my face shall not be seen."

This passage in the scriptures is more than documentation of a beautiful event. It is presented to us as a form of specific instruction. When Moses was in a state of transfiguration, there was no difficulty being in the presence of God. However, in this instance Moses, as a natural man, witnessed the appearance of the Lord after the fulness of His glory passed by. This is a most important point in the clarification of the circumstances pertaining to how we may witness the Lord.

Of equal importance, we have been instructed, and we must recognize and remember, that these appearances of Christ were prior to his mortal birth and crucifixion. He had not yet received a mortal, physical body. What was seen was His spirit. And His spirit was in the personage of a man. It is the same for our spirit prior to our mortal birth. Once again, and established in the very beginning of recorded time, God has given and caused to be recorded instructions clarifying where we came from and in what form, through the Exemplar.

Our spirits were born, grew, and developed to full stature in the premortal world, the world called heaven where God dwells.

Are we not made in God's image? Our spirits are most certainly in the personage of men and women as evidenced above. Our spirits embody who we are. Our body or image is like God's. Genesis 1:27 notes that "God created man in his own image, in the image of God created he him; male and female created he them."

We are created in God's image both spiritually *and* physically.

And to further attest to the ability to see God and live, refer to the New Testament. If a man is "in the spirit," meaning under the divine protection of God, all things can be made manifest to him.

We have only to look to the account of the martyrdom of Stephen in Acts 7:55–56, where we read, "But he [Stephen], being full of the Holy Ghost, looked up steadfastly into heaven, and saw the glory of God, and Jesus standing on the right hand of God, and said, Behold, I see the heavens opened, and the Son of man standing on the right hand of God."

How clear and succinct! There is no veiled allusion as to what transpired. There is no ambiguity or equivocation. There is simply a quotation of a declarative statement of an event that was in the process of unfolding. The transfiguration and subsequent vision of Stephen is one of the most crucial recordings in all of scripture. It explodes the myth that no one can look upon God the Father and live. It also proves that Heavenly Father and Jesus Christ are two separate and distinct individuals. Also, adding further veracity as to what took place, this event was witnessed by many people, including Saul who later became the Apostle Paul.

And there is no more telling account of a witness of the appearance of Christ than that of John the Revelator. John states in Revelation 1:17 that he sees Christ and falls at the Savior's feet as if dead. Christ lays His hand upon John and tells him to fear not, that He, Christ, is the first and the last.

There are many scriptures that attest to the fact that God is the Father of our spirits and that we are truly His children. A few are listed below:

"And Moses spake unto the Lord, saying, Let the Lord, the God of the spirits of all flesh" (Numbers 27:15–16).

"Ye are the children of the Lord your God" (Deuteronomy 14:1).

"I have said, Ye are gods; and all of you are children of the most High" (Psalm 82:6).

"Ye are the sons of the living God" (Hosea 1:10).

"Be ye therefore perfect, even as your Father which is in heaven is perfect" (Matthew 5:48).

"Forasmuch then as we are the offspring of God" (Acts 17:29).

"The Spirit itself beareth witness with our spirit, that we are the children of God" (Romans 8:16).

"Furthermore we have had fathers of our flesh which corrected us, and we gave them reverence: shall we not much rather be in subjection unto the Father of spirits, and live?" (Hebrews 12:9).

In our Heavenly Father's perfect love for us, we see that He has made Himself manifest unto us both before Christ's birth and after. To see Christ is to see the Father. God's promises are true. He has shown us, in accordance with His promise, that He is the same yesterday, today, and tomorrow.

Christ, given to us as the perfect example, has manifested Himself to us both in His spirit form, His physical form, and His resurrected form. He has shown us what we were and what we are.

Most important, He has shown us what we may become.

chapter nine

THE PREMORTAL EXISTENCE

And the angels which kept not their first estate, but left their own habitation, he hath reserved in everlasting chains under darkness unto the judgment of the great day.

—Jude 1:6

I love this beautiful little scripture. It is short in length and voluminous in content and inference. It speaks of where we lived prior to our mortal birth. It speaks of whom we lived with. It speaks of judgment based upon our choices and actions. It tells us that some of us kept our first estate and some of us did not. It tells us we lived with our Father as angels. Do we not call our children angels? Where might that expression have come from? My feeling is that it is remembered from the past.

The premortal existence is actually quite like the world in which we now live, although with certain exceptions. There, we lived with God.

Just as we grow from childhood to maturity in this earthly life, so we did in the premortal existence. We learned and developed. We gained knowledge and wisdom. We were taught the most important aspects of life and living. We were instructed what we must do to be successful in the premortal life, during our mortal life, and in life after death. We were taught correct values, virtues, and principles. We were taught the plan of salvation in its entirety. We were taught, above all, to love one another as we loved ourselves.

Some learned faster than others. Some learned better than others. Some learned more than others. But at some particular time, every one of us who has ever been on the face of the earth progressed to the point where a separation from God and a mortal body was required.

We were presented His plan for our salvation while in His presence. We were given the chance to agree or disagree with that plan and the opportunity to choose for ourselves which course of action we would follow. And we were given all facets of His plan with complete clarity of detail and consequences.

Can you imagine how wonderful it must have been to grow and develop from our spiritual birth through childhood and adolescence and then to maturity in God's presence? How wonderful it must have been to have received perfect instructions. And how sad we must have felt to see so many of our brothers and sisters make such tragic and incorrect choices.

Our Heavenly Father gave and continues to give us perfect instructions, guidance, and leadership. Yet, He allows us to choose for ourselves whether or not we will follow His directions. It can be no other way. If it were not so, His will would be forced upon us, and the chance for true learning would be eliminated. Without choice and consequences, we would never know good from evil, right from wrong, pain from pleasure. We could never truly act for ourselves. We would never have moral agency to affect a free choice. We could never possess the attributes of God and carry personal experience into the coming estates.

His plan is simple enough, but just as we see poor choices demonstrated by people today, spirits in the premortal existence also made poor choices. We may wonder how this can be. How could anybody make a poor choice in the presence of God? Again, by way of example, we return to Christ. Poor choices were made in His presence by His faithful followers, as well as those who did not believe Him. Haven't we exercised our agency in a manner that was not in accordance with the knowledge and guidance our mothers and fathers possessed? Do our children always listen to our good advice? We can see that it was the same in the premortal existence. As a consequence of moral agency, and due to pride and personal desires, some did not agree with Heavenly Father's plan. The lead proponent and spokesman for this faction was Lucifer, and many fell under the spell of his logic and influence and fallacious reasoning. Some strongly supported him, some were in moderate agreement, and others were apathetic as to either side and simply followed his crowd.

At an appropriate time and for some length of duration, there was a council in heaven (*Teachings*, 348–49), and God's plan for our salvation was the topic of concern. A leader to represent this plan in mortality was to be chosen. We were all engaged in these discussions. All premortal spirits took part. The debate was heated. Correct and incorrect reasoning was bashed back and forth as only possible in an arena where free choice is the rule. The subject of the debate was how God's plan would be implemented on earth. There were some who wanted to modify His plan.

There was a proponent of agency and free will and a proponent of enforced action. On the one hand, if we were left to choose for ourselves whether or not to follow the commandments of God, it was obvious that many souls would make incorrect choices and, therefore, not return to Heavenly Father's presence. On the other hand, if freedom of will, choice, and agency were thwarted, all would be able to return. Not a single person would be lost. But that return would not be under honest and honorable circumstances.

A great contention arose. Lines were drawn, and the battle was joined. Ideas fought ideas, reason fought reason, and we aligned ourselves on one side or the other.

In any great war, a supreme commander is chosen, and it was no different in this one. Lucifer commanded the proponents of forced acceptance. Michael led those for moral agency and choice, honesty, and honor.

In a final determination of our positions of choice, one-third of the hosts of heaven, God's children, our brothers and sisters, followed Lucifer. The rest of us supported and aligned with Jehovah.

The purpose of this council was not for us to choose who would represent our desires; rather it was whose desire we would represent. It was our opportunity to correctly exercise our agency in support of Heavenly Father and Jesus Christ. The choice of who would represent us was God's and His alone. He would accept a volunteer to carry out His will.

To determine who would implement His plan, the leaders of each side petitioned Elohim. Lucifer, not only wanting to change God's plan by eliminating our agency, sought for his own glory as well, much to his detriment.

> How art thou fallen from heaven, O Lucifer, son of the morning! How art thou cut down to the ground, which didst weaken the nations! For thou hast said in thine heart, I will ascend into heaven, I will exalt my throne above the stars of God: I will sit also upon the mount of the congregation, in sides of the north: I will ascend above the heights of the clouds; I will be like the most High. Yet thou shalt be brought down to hell, to the sides of the pit. (Isaiah 14:12–15)

Jehovah sought only for the glory of God. In speaking to the Jews during His mortal ministry, Christ established the source of His current doctrine as well as clarifying His position in the premortal existence. That He sought and seeks only for the glory of Heavenly Father, and that others should seek the same, is presented to us in John 7:16–18:

> Jesus answered them, and said, My doctrine is not mine, but his that sent me. If any man will do his will, he shall know of the doctrine, whether it be of God, or whether I speak of myself. He that speaketh of himself seeketh his own glory: but he that seeketh his glory that sent him, the same is true, and no unrighteousness is in him.

What transpired in this Grand Council is spoken of as a war in Revelation 12:7–9:

> And there was war in heaven: Michael and his angels fought against the dragon; and the dragon fought and his angels, and prevailed not; neither was their place found any more in heaven. And the great dragon was cast out, that old serpent, called the Devil, and Satan, which deceiveth the whole world: he was cast out into the earth, and his angels were cast out with him.

As for those who aligned themselves with Lucifer, Revelation 12:4 reveals more: "And his tail drew the third part of the stars of heaven, and did cast them to the earth: and the dragon stood before the woman which was ready to be delivered, for to devour her child as soon as it was born."

We see that the a third of our spirit brothers and sisters, angels who chose to follow Lucifer, those who kept not their first estate, were cast out of heaven. They, along with Lucifer, were denied a mortal, physical body. For all eternity, they would not be allowed further progression.

As for Christ, He received His birthright. That birthright, gained through obedience, is to be an heir of all that our Heavenly Father possesses. He will have *all* His Father hath—all the creations, all the worlds, all the stars and the heavens. And, as stated in the Abrahamic covenant in Genesis 22:15–18, He will have an "endless posterity," just as our Heavenly Father has.

But what of us lowly mortals? Do we have a reward? Do we deserve a reward? If we are allowed a reward, how is it obtained?

God will reward us in many ways, based upon our faithfulness in obeying His laws. For those who earnestly endeavor to keep his commandments throughout their lives, He has promised us blessings beyond measure.

In Paul's epistle to the Romans, we are instructed, among other things, that the law of Christ brings life and peace. He also states that those adopted sons of God become joint-heirs with Christ as recorded in Romans 8:14–17:

> For as many as are led by the Spirit of God, they are the sons of God. For ye have not received the spirit of bondage again to fear; but ye have received the spirit of adoption, whereby we cry, Abba, Father. The Spirit itself beareth witness with our spirit, that we are the children of God: and if children, then heirs; heirs of God, and joint-heirs with him, that we may be also glorified together.

What a wonderful and magnificent promise—to be joint-heirs with Christ, to receive all that the Father hath. To spend eternity with our Heavenly Father and Jesus Christ.

But then the thoughts creep in. If we have to be perfected, as was Christ (because I know no unclean thing can enter the kingdom of God, and to be unclean is to remain in sin, so I must have to be sinless as was Christ), to be a joint-heir, and we cannot as mortals be perfected in this life, when will we receive perfection? Doesn't that mean I have to be perfected after I die?

But, I thought if I lived a good life and believed in God and Jesus I would go to heaven. But I can't enter heaven where God and Jesus live unless I am perfected.

Will we ever receive perfection? Where? How? The scriptures state if we are led by the Spirit of God, we can be a joint-heir. Do we simply have to believe in Christ? But what of the people who lead rotten lives! Is there deathbed repentance? What of the thieves on the cross?

Am I wasting my time by keeping the commandments when I could go out and sin and have fun, and then repent and believe and be saved? I seem to remember that we are saved by grace, but I also remember that faith without works is dead. If I do no works, do I have no inheritance? Are we then saved by our works? But the scriptures say we cannot be saved by our works.

So what am I supposed to do?

SECTION IV:
OUR EARTHLY LIFE

chapter ten

THE VEIL AND THE PURPOSE
OF MORTALITY

*There is no remembrance of former things; neither shall there
be any remembrance of things that are to come with those that shall
come after.*

—Ecclesiastes 1:11

The veil is a key element to the plan of salvation. In order to make
a choice truly and freely, a choice of our own volition, we must be
separated from any undo outside influence and have no immediate and
clear recollection of our past existence. A veil has effectively been raised
between our premortal existence as spirits and our earth life. This is a
veil of forgetfulness.

Isn't it interesting that, according to scientific studies, we use
only about ten percent of our brain capacity? I can only speculate that
perhaps upon mortality that area of our brain that would allow us
those memories has been incapacitated to a large degree. In any event,
the veil is what separates our memory of what was from what is. This
allows us to begin our life with complete freedom to choose obedience
to God's instructions and ordinances or not. We find on occasion young
children sometimes relate visions and experiences that seem completely
outside the normal experiences of a child of that age. We are usually
dumbfounded when they tell us that they have seen or been comforted
by an angel.

They sometimes relate hearing the songs of heavenly choirs. They may
tell us of seeing a relative whom we know they have never been in contact
with. Most parents are at a loss to explain the nature of these events.
However, when we come to a deeper understanding of the plan of salvation and the veil of forgetfulness, a plausible explanation for these events
is offered.

Having passed through the veil of forgetfulness, we find ourselves a part of the big, wide, wonderful world. As children, we are filled with awe at all that surrounds us. One of my earliest memories serves as a monumental step in my growth and development.

I was apparently asleep as I lay on the floor. Whether this was a natural sleep of refreshing or a period of precognizance, I do not know. What I remember was looking at geometric shapes and forms. There were browns and yellows with varying shades and degrees of brightness. There were triangles and squares. They had no rhyme or reason. I did not know what they were. They were two-dimensional, and they were flat. The shapes contained no information.

I pondered what I was seeing. There was no meaning to what I saw, and it was a perplexing situation. Something in me was awakening and confronting this monumental issue before me. I could make no sense of what I was seeing. I was uncomfortable because this seemed to be out of order. Either I could not place this situation within the parameters of prior experiences, or I was becoming cognizant for the first time.

In any event, as I lay there and tried to solve this mystery, the most amazing event occurred. The two-dimensional shapes began a metamorphosis. They seemed to move, and the element of space was added to the equation. The shapes began to take on depth. Suddenly, like pieces of a puzzle joining together without any outside assistance, the disjointed planes coalesced to become the bottom, legs, and supports of a chair. I experienced either instant awareness or recognition. What I had been pondering suddenly made sense. There was comfort in this newfound knowledge. With the addition of space, depth, and perspective, the unknown and seemingly unrelated elements of the mystery were solved.

I relate this experience because it is analogous to our understanding of the events of this mortal life. It is impossible to make any sense of why things are the way they are if we do not have all the information at hand. Now, the truth is that we actually do have all the information we need. We have either asked the question but failed to search for the answers, we have failed to sufficiently ponder the situation, or we have not arrived at the level of development necessary for us to understand how the puzzle fits together.

In any event, it is not God's will to keep us in the dark. He would have us receive the light, and He would have us receive the truth. There can be no purpose in keeping us in ignorance. So when we ponder all the different situations and events that make up the social structure of this planet, we must always figure into the equation that these events. No matter how terrible and contrary to love, righteousness, mercy, and justice, they will seem, if we allow them to, to be for the betterment of mankind as a whole and for us as individuals.

The veil of forgetfulness is critically important. Because of it, we are able to exercise our choice and moral agency based upon our *faith*. *Faith* precedes the miracles. *Faith* becomes sure knowledge. *Faith* is the paradigm of *obedience*. How could we expect to receive all the Father has if we were not willing to be obedient?

For us to share in all Heavenly Father has, we must be able to function in a trustworthy manner independent of His presence. This required a separation from Him to prove to Him, but mostly to ourselves, that we are willing to be obedient and that obedience will be reflected in our actions.

To be able to know the true character of God, we must be able to know our true character. And this is only possible if we come to a knowledge and experience of those things that God has experienced. That is, the opportunity to choose right from wrong, to know good from evil, love from hate, correct principles from those that are incorrect. We must experience being in need and helping those in need. We must learn to love eternally. This is the road to perfection and God's will for us.

A degree or measure of perfection is possible in this life, just as it was in the premortal existence. Ultimate or complete perfection can be achieved only when we pass beyond mortality. This should be a comfort to us. We need only to do the best we can while here on earth, just as we did in premortality. The rest we can do under different circumstances at a later date.

Many things can only be experienced when we possess a physical body and live outside the presence of God. We came from a state where everything was provided for us to satisfy the requirements of living to a state where everything is provided for us, but it is only available for our acquisition through difficulty, diligence, fortitude, commitment, and, sometimes, the kindness of others. The earth was cursed for Adam's sake and for ours. We must toil for our bread and shelter. It is difficult but not bad. How could we appreciate the ease of living in the premortal and postmortal states if we had nothing to compare it to?

Opposition is necessary in all things in order for us to gain that appreciation. Trials and struggles are necessary for the development of our character. They are essential if we are to have understanding of and compassion for others and the difficulties they have experienced. Our sickness and injuries, our gains and losses, our hunger and satiation, our deprivations and wants must be experienced in order for us to mature intellectually. We must have points of comparison. We must have these trials so that we can mourn with those who mourn, as well as rejoice with those who have joy. True joy is possible only if we know true despair. To the varying degrees that we experience these points of opposition, that is the degree that we may experience the depth of our counterpoint.

We never fully appreciate how precious life is until a life is lost. We never fully appreciate the depth of love until love is lost. We never fully appreciate the worth of a soul until a soul is lost.

We must experience physical and mental pain to become whole. We must suffer never having possessed as well as loss of possessions. We must have security balanced by insecurity. For there to be true peace, there must be war. There must be justice and injustice, life and death, joy and sorrow, health and sickness. Only by experiencing a lack of forgiveness may we truly forgive. Only by giving love away may we possess love.

It is only through the existence of these opposites that we may come to know truth. It is only through an acceptance of the truths of life that all truths may become one. All of these conditions have been given to us for our sake. *Sake* is defined as advantage, behalf, and benefit. Life is a refining process. It is here that we have the opportunity to more quickly learn and develop in certain areas. Not all things were possible to learn in the premortal world, and a temporal existence not only facilitates but also expedites the process. We must understand that. Although we may not know and appreciate why we are in the midst of certain trials, they are and will be for our advantage and benefit. We are allowed experiences, trials, and temptations so we may progress.

Ultimately, the reason for this earthly life is so we may be exposed to all the above-mentioned circumstances in a compressed period of time, relative to eternity. We have this life provided for us so we may choose to live by faith and the proper exercise of moral agency, thus affecting a quicker progression toward perfection.

chapter eleven

HOW CAN GOD ALLOW THIS CRUELTY AND SUFFERING?

A God of perfect love would not arbitrarily cause people to hate one another. His commandment is to love one another. He does not sit on His throne on high and cause murder, rape, and unconscionable acts to occur to amuse Himself. He is a God of mercy and compassion. He does not cause sickness and injury to happen so that our lives will be miserable. He has healing in His hands. He does not cause misery, wars, and tragic events. But He *does* allow them to happen.

Would a merciful God take away our agency, our gift to choose for ourselves? If He did, how would we ever learn? To have our choices and their effects negated by another more powerful being was the plan of Satan, and that plan was quelled from the beginning.

An all-knowing, all-powerful, and all-loving Father will not cause harm to come to His children. He will only act in and allow events to happen that are in our best interest.

If we, in our selfish attitudes and emotions, blame our Heavenly Father for hurt we feel for what may have happened to our children or ourselves or even others, does it not stand to reason that He, the Father of us all, feels your pain and your children's pain and the pain of others to an even greater degree? Heavenly Father in not immune to the suffering and despair in our lives. He has borne the grief of *all* the worlds.

His wish for us is to live in eternal joy and happiness. In His perfect wisdom, He realizes we must endure a short time of suffering to accomplish this. And He will never let happen to us more than we can bear. He is always there for us. He is sometimes beside us and sometimes carrying us. But He will never abandon us.

In reflection on your life's experiences, do you not find that your greatest satisfaction was when you extended yourself? When you put your effort into accomplishing some goal? Is there ever a true reward without effort? When we earn something, our wages have more value.

I know it is difficult to reconcile the tragedies that occur in our lives. It is difficult to understand how God lets these things happen. Cruelty and suffering, sickness and evil are pervasive in the world. Why is this allowed?

To understand the answer, we must look to ourselves. How do we exercise our agency? What choices do we make?

I heard a young woman complain that she is unfairly going to jail. "What about my children," she says. She was trying to be a good mother and provide for them. She was selling drugs to make money so she could stay off welfare. She stated she was doing the right thing and is a victim of circumstance.

Now I ask, whose fault is it that she became pregnant at fifteen? Whose fault is it that she quit school and has no education? Whose fault is it that she can't get a job? Whose fault is it that she chose to give herself to someone outside of marriage? Whose fault is it that she has no husband? Who forced her to use and sell drugs? Who forced her into her present situation?

A smoker became ill with cancer and sued the tobacco company. The first puff taken on a cigarette causes everyone to cough. That is the body's violent reaction and expulsion of a substance that is harmful to it. Yet, this smoker continued to smoke, even though it has been common knowledge since the days of Mark Twain that smoking is addictive. If you could go back in time, you could ask anyone who had tried to quit. But, this smoker ignored all the warnings. For years, he watched people die from lung cancer, and he ignored those warnings. He ignored the warning labels on every pack he purchased. He ignored his wife's pleadings for him to quit. And just as he ignored those and other warnings, he had just as many rationalizations why he can't quit. Never mind that millions and millions have managed it; he is the one for whom it was impossible. So, he supposed it is the tobacco company's fault that he had cancer.

Then there is the alcoholic and the drug addict and the wife beater (the way she acted made him do it). There are those who forsook their education and denigrate any person who is willing to become educated.

There are liars, cheats, and thieves. There are those who war over jealousy and religion and those who fight over ideological concepts. There are those who are promiscuous and those who have no respect for others or themselves.

There are also those who are apathetic. They don't vote. They don't get involved. They let everybody else make the decisions that affect their lives and then complain when they don't like the results.

Then, there are those who make good and proper choices, those who rise above the circumstance into which they were born, those who forsake advantaged circumstances that involved untoward activities, those who value education and are willing to sacrifice to obtain it, those who value the family as paramount. There are many good, great, honest people.

We are all in this world together. Every action of mine affects another. We are the family of man. We are intertwined from birth to death. What happens in America affects Tibet. What happens in Albuquerque affects Pocatello. The choice a doctor makes may save a patient. The choice a patient makes may cause his own demise. Good people are affected by the most horrendous circumstances due to the choices made by others.

All this is simply life.

If we are to successfully negotiate our time on earth, we must accept personal responsibility for our lives and the events that circumscribe them. We cannot blame others or God. Truth be known, we should thank them. When others wrong us, we are the ones who suffer until we forgive. Of one thing we can be sure: we will never be wronged by God.

We are allowed to experience and be affected by the good and evil in this world so we may learn and grow. We are given these experiences for our benefit and that of others so that we may develop compassion and love. We are allowed trials so we may become strong. We are allowed temptations so we may resist. We are taken to the point where we feel we can take no more so we will come to rely on God. It is left to us to decide and choose how we react to these tests and trials.

We are allowed to experience reversals to crush our pride so we may become humble.

If we are humble, we are teachable. And, if we are teachable, we may gain knowledge and wisdom. If we are wise, we come to depend upon, call upon, know, and obey our Heavenly Father.

It is only through God's lack of intervention that we may gain real and true experience and achieve the measure of growth necessary for further progression.

chapter twelve

WHAT ARE WE TO DO?

Be ye therefore perfect, even as your Father which is in heaven is perfect.

—Matthew 5:48

This might seem like a pretty tall order. How on earth are we to fulfill this commandment? We know that Christ was and will be the only perfect being to inhabit our world. So God appears to be instructing us to do something that we are unable to do. Is it really possible that we may achieve perfection? Or are we being commanded to do something we cannot do?

The truth is that we can, indeed, become perfect. God will never ask us to do something we are unable to do. He always provides a way to successfully complete the tasks He has set before us. "I can do all things through Christ which strengtheneth me" (Philippians 4:13).

It may seem an obvious truth, but the perfection of Christ was achieved by being perfectly obedient to Heavenly Father and was manifested by the fact that He was without sin. The very fact that we have at one time or another sinned precludes us from Christlike perfection. We cannot be perfect in the sense that He was perfect. But Christ makes up through His atoning sacrifice for those things we are unable to overcome ourselves.

We cannot overcome sin. We may stop committing particular sins, but only through the Atonement are the effects of sin overcome. Redeeming us from our sins was part of Christ's calling and part of His perfection. We can, however, attain to the highest standards set down for us to achieve in mortality.

This would be manifested for mortals by obedience to all the laws and ordinances prescribed by our Heavenly Father. For us to be perfect, even as our Father in heaven is perfect, is for us to become fully developed spiritually. We are to be as complete and obedient as we can. We are to be finished, meaning that we are to manifest in our lives love for all mankind. We are to act with virtue. We are to be the example of values, righteousness, caring, and compassion. We are to help others in this achievement. This is the perfection we can attain in this lifetime.

We have been given the perfect example to follow. When God gave us His Son, Jesus Christ, our Heavenly Father showed us who He is through His Son. When we want to know how to act or what to do, we have only to look to Christ. He is the way, the truth, and the life. When we are commanded to be perfect as God is, we need only to turn to the perfect example. Simply examine the life of Christ by reading the scriptures, as well as examining other good works that depict His life. Accompany this with prayer, fasting, and meditation, and we can receive a witness of the Holy Ghost about how we should act and what we should do.

For many, the most prominent aspects of the life of Jesus are His crucifixion and the miracles He performed. They remember water being turned into wine. They recall the lame man walked, the lepers were cleansed, the blind saw, and the dead arose. They remember His cruel death on the cross. But most fail to see the true depth and meaning of those acts.

As our perfect example, what are we to learn from His deeds? Is our charge to alter the elements? Are we to heal the sick and raise the dead? Yes, we could do those things if that was what was important and needed. Christ admonished the apostles, "O ye of little faith" (Luke 12:28). If they had just the faith of a mustard seed, they could move mountains (see Matthew 17:20).

We are not asked to move mountains. We are only asked to do what Christ was teaching in those many examples—we are asked to serve.

A most beautiful lesson on the importance of service is recorded in Matthew 25:31–46, where those who serve are given a promise and those who choose not to serve are admonished:

> When the son of man shall come in his glory, and all the holy angels with him, then shall he sit upon the throne of his glory: and before him shall be gathered all nations: and he shall separate them one from another, as a shepherd divideth his sheep from the goats: and he shall set the sheep on his right hand, but the goats on the left.
>
> Then shall the King say unto them on his right hand, Come, ye blessed of my father, inherit the kingdom prepared for you from the foundation of the world: for I was an hungred, and ye gave me

meat: I was thirsty, and ye gave me drink: I was a stranger and ye took me in: naked, and ye clothed me: I was sick, and ye visited me: I was in prison, and ye came unto me.

Then shall the righteous answer him, saying, Lord, when saw we thee an hungred, and fed thee? or thirsty, and gave thee drink? When saw we thee a stranger, and took thee in? or naked, and clothed thee? Or when saw we thee sick, or in prison, and came unto thee?

And the King shall answer and say unto them, Verily I say unto you, Inasmuch as ye have done it unto one of the least of these my brethren, ye have done it unto me. Then shall he say also unto them on the left hand, Depart from me, ye cursed, into everlasting fire, prepared for the devil and his angels:

For I was an hungred, and ye gave me no meat: I was thirsty, and ye gave me no drink: I was a stranger, and ye took me not in: naked, and ye clothed me not: sick, and in prison, and ye visited me not. Then shall they also answer him, saying, Lord, when saw we thee an hungred, or athirst, or a stranger, or naked, or sick, or in prison, and did not minister unto thee?

Then shall he answer them, saying, Verily I say unto you, Inasmuch as ye did it not to one of the least of these, ye did it not to me. And these shall go away into everlasting punishment: but the righteous into life eternal.

One of the commandments we are asked to honor is to serve our fellow man. We are to serve them in temporal and in spiritual ways. We are exhorted in Matthew 22:39 to love our neighbor as we love ourselves. If we reflect on how we may help, the opportunities are endless. We can embark on extensive and complicated undertakings to help humanity as a whole. But, more important, we are responsible for daily acts of kindness that ultimately serve all humanity.

I have seen the joy and gratitude felt by the elderly when a group of young men clean their yard. I have seen light and happiness change the countenance of the housebound when they receive a visit. Taking in a neighbor's trash cans creates good bonds.

I remember a simple act of courtesy I performed many years ago when I was in Spain. On a short leave during my army service, I vacationed on the northeast coast of that beautiful country. In the small town of Malgrat del Mar, I approached the entrance of a shop at the same moment as did a lovely young lady. I reached the door a half step before she did and held the door open for her. A startled look came over her face as she was taken aback by this act from an American. The surprised look was replaced by a grateful and enchanting smile and the phrase, "Muchas gracias." My "De nada" was equally appreciated. This occurred in 1972. To this day, no matter where I am, when I hold the door for someone the gratitude is the same.

Have you noticed how checkout clerks at the grocery store light up when you direct a pleasant comment to them? And how the acknowledgment of a person's attire brings a moment of happiness? We may serve each other in a thousand ways, from a simple compliment to assistance with a neighbor's needs. We may run an errand or loan our car. We may help move a piece of furniture. We may inquire if something seems to be amiss at their home. We can teach children. We can serve the community on a special day of volunteer activity with our church group or as individuals. We can lend a nonjudgmental ear to those struggling with the weight of their trials.

We need to be there for each other whenever the opportunity arises. We need to help others by letting them help us. We need to break down our pride and accept assistance when it is warranted. Not to do so robs our friends of the joy and blessings that service brings into their lives.

That is what God wants us to know—that although service is a wonderful benefit for others, when we serve, the greatest benefit is ours. Heavenly Father, in His infinite and perfect love, blesses us more richly for an act of kindness we provide for one of our brothers and sisters than that act provides assistance to others.

How deeply important and dear to Heavenly Father are His children. How great the love and compassion He has for us. He would have us take care of each other as He would care for us if we were in His presence. There is a great lesson to be learned in this commandment. We see the importance of temporal service toward each other. We see how we may assist God in the care of His children by providing help that He himself will not directly do.

He helps us with our needs through our mutual assistance. But because of the constraints He has placed upon Himself, He will not directly intervene and force us to serve. To do so would be to violate our free will. Only if no other way exists will He provide a miracle to ameliorate a specific situation. Are we coming to an understanding of the precious nature of our agency? Do we not see that God must honor the parameters of mortality that He framed?

We must come to a complete and thorough realization of the importance of caring for one another. God cannot directly step in and change the consequences of our choices. It would violate the laws He instituted and the plan of salvation. For Him to alter the effects of our actions would negate the choices we made in the premortal existence, as well as the choices we make in mortality and our opportunity for progression. To become as He is, we must choose for ourselves, reap what we sow, and learn from our decisions and actions.

"Blessed is the man that walketh not in the counsel of the ungodly, nor standeth in the way of sinners, nor sitteth in the seat of the scornful. But his delight is in the law of the Lord; and in his law doth he meditate day and night" (Psalm 1:1–2).

Our understanding of, and obedience to, God's law is the key element of our judgment.

It would serve us well to meditate upon the law of the Lord. We would be wise to study the scriptures for what is written by the prophets on this subject. We would be wise indeed to come to an understanding of the consequences of our actions appertaining to His laws.

We often hear reference made to following the commandments listed in Exodus 20. The Ten Commandments are usually understood as not only being all-inclusive but also the sum total of what we are to do and how we are to act. However, these rules of conduct are provided as a basic starting point for what we are to do, and they delineate, for the most part, matters concerning temporal behavior. The instructions are only a starting point from which spring many other spiritual as well as temporal commandments. The original Ten Commandments are basic, broad in scope, and leave room for greater depth and refinement.

Moses came down from the mount the second time with a set of temporal instructions from God. As His messenger, Moses received revelation that governed the day-to-day actions of the Israelite nation. This chosen people were continually being taught of the coming of the kingdom of God and the appearance of their deliverer. The instructions concerning their temporal conduct was given to guide them (and us) to behave in a manner consistent with the Godlike qualities necessary to live in a state of exaltation.

Their spiritual doctrines, including ritual animal sacrifice, were conducted to be a type, or similitude, of the coming Savior. Upon this group fell the blessings and responsibility of preparing the way for the

coming of the Lord. Lands were prepared, correct behavior was instituted, reliance upon a prophet to disseminate the instructions of God was
established, rules of worship were set forth, moral agency was effected,
and the consequences of straying from correct principles and actions were
enacted. The people were given trials to test their faithfulness. Only by
exhibiting the necessary faith were they allowed to proceed in temporal
and spiritual growth. Israel was blessed, and they were chastised. The
Lord will discipline, rebuke, chastise, and punish those whom He loves.

Are not the best parents those who set proper limits of behavior
and conduct and explain the consequences and ramifications of actions
that stray outside the bounds that they have set? Do not the best parents
then, in love, discipline their children when they fail to obey those rules
prescribed to facilitate their greatest growth and potential and the growth
and potential of the others they affect? We should never forget that the
punishments of God are just and merciful and as lenient as God's law
allows. They are always given in perfect love and for our benefit.

A lovely verse in James 2:5 reads, "Hearken, my beloved brethren,
Hath not God chosen the poor of this world rich in faith, and heirs of the
kingdom which he hath promised to them that love him?"

Of course, not only must we be rich in faith to be a joint-heir with
Christ, but we must also love God. The way we show our love for God
is by keeping all His commandments. The ordinances given to us are
commandments. The words that proceed forth from the mouth of Christ
are commandments. His admonitions and exhortations are commandments. He has commanded us to have faith, be baptized, and receive the
Holy Ghost by a legal, authorized administrator; serve our fellow man in
humility; become as children; become humble at all times and in all ways;
exercise good works; pray and ponder; partake of the sacrament; and love
one another even as He has loved us. These are only a few commandments
that have been set forth.

When we think of the commandments, we often have a companion
thought. Sin. It is a word that strikes a certain amount of consternation,
resignation, hopelessness, despair, and even an element of terror in our
hearts. It seems unconquerable. It seems to be the great stumbling block
to our salvation. With all the ways we may sin, it appears insurmountable,
and most people seem to have succumbed to a quiet resignation of their
inability to overcome sin and its effects. But knowledge is power. We have
been given all the power necessary to eliminate as much sin from our

lives as humanly possible. We are and always will be sinners by virtue of the fact that we have all committed sin at some period in our life. Yet, we must strive to become as sinless as possible in our future actions.

To begin our efforts at overcoming sin to the best of our ability, we can divide sin into two categories: sins of omission and sins of commission. When we have neglected to perform a commanded act, such as being baptized, receiving the Holy Ghost, praying or serving one another, we have committed a sin of omission. We have simply not followed through in doing a prescribed act.

When we forthrightly and directly act in a manner contrary to the commandments, we have engaged in a sin of commission. Examples include adultery, lying, stealing, murder, not honoring our parents, and so forth. Sins of commission can lead to sins of omission. If we regularly attend our church services but oversleep and awake after the services are over, we have committed a sin of omission. Now if it felt so good to sleep in on that Sabbath day and we choose to do it the following week, we have fallen into a sin of commission. Engaging in sins of commission require much greater volition or willingness on our part than committing sins of omission.

Obtaining perfection is a necessary requirement for our exaltation and for us to live with our Heavenly Father. It is often stated that no unclean thing can enter the kingdom of heaven. Again, it seems a contradiction arises because we know that we are not without sin, and therefore, we are unclean. We have sinned in the past, and it is most likely we will sin in the future. Try as we might, we will commit a sin of either omission or commission. We will treat someone poorly, or we may be inappropriate in our administration of justice or punishment toward our children. We may speak badly about someone. We may fail to attend church services, or we may neglect our daily prayers.

There are a thousand ways both large and small that we will err. We are promised to be joint-heirs with Christ, but we must become sinless and perfect. It would be a mistake to entertain the thought that upon passing from this mortal life, we instantly attain perfection. Our agency, or freedom to choose, has been a gift from the beginning of time and will continue so throughout eternity. When we pass beyond this mortal existence, we will still have the freedom to choose. After mortality, the choices laid before us will be those that are in accordance with the teachings and precepts of God, thus bringing us closer to Him, or they will be choices at odds with His plan for our salvation and will lead us away from Him. If we choose the latter, we will have committed a sin either of omission or commission. The effect will be to separate us from those individuals whose choices allow them to receive the eternal blessings of living in exaltation.

As we consider these final events that lead to our eternal reward, we will see how those individual threads, those various parts of His plan for our salvation, are woven together into a beautiful tapestry depicting the glory of exaltation.

There will be a coming together of individual agency and circumstance; supernal and mortal desire; law and justice; justice and mercy; love and effort; comfort and compassion. We will see that God gives no command, or law, to His children without providing a way for them to accomplish it.

Knowing that with God there can be no contradictions, we understand that He must have provided a way for sin to be overcome. The way provided was through the Atonement of Jesus Christ. "Jesus saith unto him, I am the way the truth and the life: no man cometh unto the Father, but by me" (John 14:6).

For the Atonement to be fully efficacious requires an effort on our part. We must repent of the sins we have committed and continue to repent on an ongoing basis.

How thankful I am for the great gift of repentance. As I continue to grow and stumble and make mistakes, I know that if I offer a broken heart and contrite spirit for the sins and transgressions I commit, coupled with sincere effort to never commit them again, my Father in heaven will forgive me. He will wipe the slate clean and once again give me the opportunity to right my wrongs and write my recommendation in the book of life.

Repentance is a most wonderful gift, and although true repentance can be a terribly painful experience, the rewards and blessings we receive from this act of contrition are quite disproportionate to the discomfort we feel during this act of humility. For us to truly engage in the act of repentance, we must come before the Lord with a broken heart and a contrite spirit. There must be a sincere desire to stop the errant behavior and discontinue its practice in the future. There is pain in repentance. Often tears are shed. There is anguish in the soul. We feel terribly unworthy to receive His love, for we come to a sudden and sure understanding that what we have done is contrary to His will. We feel we have shamed ourselves before Him. We realize that even though we may have committed the most despicable sin, He has always been there for us and is willing to forgive us. We realize the small, petty and selfish nature of our actions.

We know how much we depend on Him and how He has always been there for us at all times and in all places and how we have abandoned His teachings and love. We realize that our choices have placed us where we are. We also realize that God is there for us still, no matter how badly we have behaved. But we must come to Him. He stands with open arms waiting for our return. He wants to gather us under the protection of His wings, as a mother bird does her chicks, and provide us with comfort and peace. Because He paid a price for us, we too must pay a price. We must truly repent.

To repent is to become humble. It is to bow our knee before Christ and declare Him the Master. To be humble is to place the wants and desires of God and others before our own. Now God, being perfect, has already placed our needs before His. Is this not also the case with our children and us? Do we not serve them and place their needs above ours? So too it is with God, though His love and service is magnified to an incomprehensible degree.

Whatever we do for or give to our Heavenly Father, we receive back in far greater measure than what was spent through our efforts. We can never repay all that is given us. But we must repay all that we can. And so, in the act of repentance, we must be sorry for what we did. We must be contrite. We must confess our unworthy actions to God, make restitution to those whom we offended, make a sincere effort never to repeat the action, and place ourselves before our Father in humility.

Do not despair at all that is entailed and implied in this discussion of repentance. Were it not in our best interest, God would not have instituted it. It is paramount to remember at this juncture that we can never be perfect in mortality, and that is all right. We were never meant to be perfect at this stage in our development. If such were the case, there would be no need for a Savior. It would negate the need for the Atonement and would invalidate the plan of salvation. We could throw out all the writings about the necessity of, and the coming of, Christ. There would have been no war in heaven concerning who would represent God's plan for us.

We are not perfect during this life and cannot be. The good news is that one perfect being, Christ, provided for that which we are unable to do ourselves. We should thank God every day and night for His love, the love of His Son, and the wonderful blessing of repentance. Christ will overcome our sins and fulfill the demands of justice with His mercy. We are only asked to obey to the best of our ability.

We are the only factor that can prevent us from fulfilling the desires God has for our exaltation. The only negating factor that will exclude us from exaltation is the manner in which we exercise our moral agency. After all, the choices we make in mortality determine our reward in eternity.

Great blessings come about through repentance. We are forgiven of our sins and transgressions. We gain peace in our soul. We have a promise of the future. We have someone upon whom we may lean. We are given strength beyond our own. We are loved and are given to know of His love for us. We realize how precious we are in the sight of God and how precious are all those about us. We can strengthen relationships. We can be forgiven. We will forgive others. We are given a keen insight into the personality of God and godhood. We learn about justice, and we learn about mercy. Most of all, we see the necessity of humility, and we learn how to become humble.

Humility is what places us on that straight and narrow path leading to exaltation. Being humble allows us to be teachable. God cannot teach us if we are not willing to be taught. If we choose to be stiffnecked and proud, we cannot be taught, and thus we turn our backs upon the love and mercy of God. Our correct, proper choices lead us back to our Father one step at a time.

When our spiritual growth has progressed to encompass the first and second principles of the gospel, faith and repentance, we are ready to place ourselves in the hands of Christ and submit to the ordinances He has set forth for our exaltation.

An ordinance is:

1. A direction or command of an authoritative nature.

2. A custom or practice established by usage or authority.

3. An established religious rite; specifically, the Communion.

In our day-to-day living, we are continually affected by ordinances. These are the laws established by man to govern our social interaction, so we may have order in our temporal associations. These ordinances are our laws. They set forth rules of conduct with a reward and penalty for their observance or lack of their observance. If we obey the law, we can function in a safe, courteous, ordered fashion. We will not intrude upon others' rights, and they will not intrude on ours. We will have peace, harmony and safety as the rewards for obedience to those ordinances. Those are the rewards.

On the other hand, if we choose not to obey the laws, we bring disorder, discourtesy, disrespect, discordance, and danger to ourselves and others, the result of which is the degradation of society and the degradation of ourselves. When we fail to obey the ordinances agreed upon and set as a standard by society, we bring upon ourselves the justice that society demands. We are punished for the incorrect exercise of our agency.

We may pay a small fine and continue with our normal lives. We may suffer a more serious punishment, based upon our actions, that may alter our lives forever. The severity of our misdeeds may even place us in a position where we will never be able to improve the conditions imposed upon us due to the choice we made.

We have the opportunity on a daily basis to exercise our moral agency in a correct or incorrect manner with consequences that will affect the rest of our mortal existence. Likewise, we face daily choices that will effect not only on our temporal existence but our existence for all time and eternity.

There are laws of man and the laws of God. Most of the laws and ordinances that delineate our social mores and daily social conduct, with their attendant rewards and punishments, are taken from the Ten Commandments and are implemented in some form or other. Some or all of the Ten Commandments form the basis of most societal structure. Even though these are the basic laws, or ordinances, instituted by God, they are man's laws by virtue of the fact that they have been fashioned to fit each particular society's needs and cultural values. Various social structures through the interpretation of whichever ruling party is in power at the time will accept or reject some or all of God's commands.

On the most basic level, the rules of conduct, or commandments, were set forth to govern the temporal aspects of life. Of course, the ultimate purpose of His commandments is to guide us in our daily actions so that we might correctly exercise choice in the manner in which we live so that we may, one day, return to and live in His presence.

There is no equivocation with respect to God's laws or ordinances. They are basic, pure, and simple. They are not open to change, so as to fit the whims of the prevailing social attitude of the time. A perfect being created perfect laws. It is as simple as that. Heavenly Father does not shroud His intentions in a cloak of vague and ambiguous statements. Satan will lie blatantly.

Of greater danger are the subtle lies that Satan spreads. He will envelope a lie with enough truth to make it appear to be something that it is not. In the current vernacular, this is called spin. Satan is a master spinner. From the beginning of time, he has spun enough thread to weave a blanket of lies and deception to cover the world. He will include in his lies enough truth to make those lies seem plausible.

However, God has turned the tables on this fallen son. God will allow all events in our lives, good or bad, to bring us to Him if we use those tools He has given us. These are the tools of discernment and reason. If we base all our reasoning on the premise that Heavenly Father and Jesus Christ embody perfection, that their plans are flawless, that their instructions are without fault, and that their laws and ordinances are without peer, then we will be able to discern correct from incorrect principles. We will determine correct from incorrect reasoning. We will rend the shroud of lies and ambiguity that have been perpetrated by Satan and his followers. We will come to know God's plan for us in all its majesty and glory. We will see how man has intentionally and unintentionally perverted the beautiful purposes and reasons of and for our Heavenly Father's ordinances.

We have been given a choice of who to follow. It is our responsibility to learn the truth. This is the desire of God, for the truth shall set you free.

Consider the following scriptural admonition: "They that forsake the law praise the wicked: but such as keep the law contend with them. Evil men understand not judgment: but they that seek the Lord understand all things. Better is the poor that walketh in his uprightness, than he that is perverse in his ways, though he be rich" (Proverbs 28:4–6).

Because He is fair and just, Heavenly Father will not establish different rules of conduct or different laws necessary for exaltation based on which nation a person lives in or what a person's individual circumstances are. Nor would he vary the rules within nations. His laws are eternal and unchanging. He will not respect one nation over another or one person over another. Heavenly Father is no respecter of persons.

It is said that one man's meat is another man's poison. In the gospel perspective, it is more difficult for a rich man to enter the kingdom of heaven than a man who is poor. The rich are swallowed up in the trappings of wealth. This is Satan's playground. How much more difficult for the rich to rely upon God and the Holy Spirit than for the poor. Blessed are the poor. How much easier for them to depend on faith. How much more blessed are they for the personal relationship with the Savior they may develop through the circumstances of their lives than the rich who rely on the strength of their own arm.

With all of our temporal needs fulfilled, we rarely acquire that deep hunger for spiritual fulfillment. If the wealthy do hunger for spiritual enlightenment, how much more difficult for them to leave the security of the trappings of their earthly riches for something that seems vague and at best only a hope? They have a longer road to travel to obtain the first principle of the gospel, faith, than those who have that principle thrust upon them by temporal necessity throughout their lives.

Truly blessed are the poor. And what a curse can be riches.

Yet, regardless of the circumstances of life, God has allowed the individual circumstances of each person's life to be that which will ultimately bless him the most.

Through the act of conformation, all aspects of the gospel reveal their deeper meanings as we become more spiritually mature. That is why we can read the Bible over and over and still find new personal revelations in old scripture. It is not the teachings, principles, and ordinances that change; it is our understanding of their meanings and inferences that grows and develops. This is how we are edified (instructed morally or spiritually), line upon line and precept upon precept. We once saw through a glass darkly (see 1 Corinthians 13:12), but as the gospel light begins to illuminate our intellect, we are blessed with greater clarity of what God is trying to teach us. The veil between the temporal and the eternal thins. As we grow, we experience a greater appreciation and love not only for God and Jesus Christ but also for the beautiful and simple teachings contained in the scriptures.

We begin to truly understand why God asks us to do certain things. We begin to focus not on ourselves and our salvation but upon others and their salvation. We start to become selfless. We begin to serve our fellow man, not just to guarantee our salvation, or even to please God, but for the pure desire to serve our brothers and sisters throughout the world. We take ourselves out of the equation because of our love for all our Heavenly Father's children. We desire others to receive all the blessings that are theirs for the taking. We want them to have the peace and comfort that we have received from becoming humble, willing, and obedient in following God's plan.

chapter thirteen

BAPTISM AND RECEIVING THE HOLY GHOST

One Lord, one faith, one baptism.

—Ephesians 4:6

This most gentle and beautiful ordinance of baptism is undoubtedly the most perfect and appropriate act we can undertake to demonstrate one's beginning commitment to following the teachings of God the Father and Jesus Christ.

Baptism is many things. It is symbolic and it is pragmatic. It allows us to begin to understand Christ's Atonement as well as cleansing us of our sins. At baptism we make our first covenants with Heavenly Father. Baptism is an act that shows our willingness and desire to become humble and to place ourselves in the hands of a higher authority. We are demonstrating our willingness to undertake all the trials, tribulations, and the responsibilities of becoming a new person; of being born again; of striving to be perfect as our Father in heaven is perfect; of becoming a person who will eschew the prevailing whims, capriciousness, and petulance of our ever-changing society.

When we are baptized, we anchor ourselves to the everlasting gospel, never again to be tossed to and fro by the latest interpretation of religion or to be captured by a religion that changes depending on what is popular, politically correct, or in vogue. God will not change the necessary ordinances that He instituted from the beginning of time simply to appease the whims of a confused society.

At first blush, it seems that we are baptized merely as an outward demonstration of accepting Christ as our Savior. That is partially correct. At some point prior to being baptized, we question and examine what baptism is. It is at this point that we become aware of the true significance and symbolism of baptism as well as who may perform this most sacred ordinance in accordance with the laws established by God and Jesus Christ.

It follows simple logic that if God requires baptism, then He would specify the manner in which it is to be performed. It also follows that He would leave those instructions in the scriptures. Through prayer, study, meditation, and personal revelation, the importance of this first ordinance and who is given the authority to perform it reveals itself.

Baptism is of supreme importance. It is the first step along the straight and narrow path that leads to exaltation. Contrary to how it is generally perceived, the straight and narrow path is not intended to, nor does it make life more difficult. If we desire to travel from point A to point B, the most wearisome road is a wide, circuitous route, although this is the route most of us take. We usually choose the route of man rather than the route of God.

Imagine bouncing from side to side and winding back and forth for mile after mile. Your goal is in sight, but the road you are taking (the road of man) requires you to travel a thousand times further than the path you did not choose. Now which is easier: man's path or the one that is narrow to keep us safely within its confines and straight so as to lead us most directly and quickly to our goal? The answer is obvious. And the good news is that if we have taken the wrong path, God has provided a detour that will immediately place us on the proper road.

This initial ordinance of baptism and its importance cannot be more clearly taught to us than by reading the exchange that takes place between John the Baptist and the detractors of Christ, as well as the exchange that occurs between John and Christ Himself.

One segment of the Jews who opposed Christ was the Pharisees. They were a separatist faction of the Jews and a major hindrance to the acceptance of Christ and His teachings. They were given to ritual observance of the letter of the law and rules of religious conduct and generally failed to recognize the spirit in which the law was intended. The Pharisees were much given to spiritual pride, which indicates a lack of dependence on the Lord and an unwillingness to be edified.

The Sadducees were a faction who formed the small yet powerful Jewish aristocracy. They were in opposition to the Lord, among other things, because of His cleansing of the temple of the money changers. They did not believe the Lord was resurrected, and they worked to thwart the ministry of Christ's apostles.

It is to these nonbelievers that John the Baptist made this address recorded in Matthew:

> But when he saw many of the Pharisees and Sadducees come to his baptism, he said unto them, O generation of vipers, who hath warned you to flee from the wrath to come? Bring forth therefore fruits meet for repentance:
>
> And think not to say within yourselves, We have Abraham to our Father: for I say unto you, that God is able of these stones to raise up children unto Abraham. And now also the axe is laid unto the root of the trees: therefore every tree which bringeth not forth good fruit is hewn down, and cast into the fire. I indeed baptize you with water unto repentance: but he that cometh after me is mightier than I, whose shoes I am not worthy to bear: he shall baptize you with the Holy Ghost, and with fire:
>
> Whose fan is in his hand, and he will thoroughly purge his floor, and gather his wheat into the garner: but he will burn up the chaff with unquenchable fire. (Matthew 3:7–12)

This is a mighty admonition to the proud and unbelieving as well as a call to repentance. It is a warning of the fate to come for those who fail to heed the prophecies of times past and present. John points out their arrogance and pride and how they, through their social standing and authoritative positions, have poisoned those of their generation, a "generation of vipers." Do not miss this symbolism. Not only does the snake represent Satan and his works and desires, but a viper is poisonous. They are poisoning the people causing them a spiritual death.

In asking His question, "Who hath warned you to flee from the wrath to come?" (Matthew 3:7), he is reminding them of the warnings of the prophets that have been issued to God's chosen people from the beginning of time. He is bringing to their remembrance the true written word and oral instructions they, and those of prior generations, have received. John knows the stumbling block of their pride in being descendants of Abraham. He reminds them that God can choose whomsoever he desires to receive the Abrahamic covenant and that unless they humble themselves and come to a true understanding of the law and avail themselves of God's plan for their salvation, they will be denied the blessings of exaltation.

We can imagine the shock and horror these Jews felt as John went on to tell what fate lies before them if they do not repent. He used the imagery of something with which they are familiar: an image of a tree in an orchard.

When a tree in an orchard ceases to produce fruit that is of benefit to its owner, it is cut down and burned. It is destroyed. It serves no purpose and is cast out, never again to be in the presence of the other trees or its owner. It will never again be pruned and receive care. It will never again be nurtured. It will receive no sustenance. Its existence will be eternally changed, never again to grow or have an increase.

John then points out that they have a choice. They can repent and be baptized. They can be cleansed by the fire of the Holy Ghost, or they can be destroyed by the fire of the almighty God. They can be gathered in as wheat, or they can be burned as the chaff after the harvest. They may live in the garner (a garner is a storehouse for grain; grain symbolizes the children of God whom He takes into His mansions) or be swept away from His presence. If the Israelites choose to be swept away, they will live with the eternal pain of self-reproach that burns as a fire.

John makes quite a strong case for the necessity of baptism, but as we will see, his case gets even stronger.

> Then cometh Jesus from Galilee to Jordan unto John, to be baptized of him. But John forbad him, saying, I have need to be baptized of thee, and comest thou to me? And Jesus answering said unto him, Suffer it to be so now: for thus it becometh us to fulfil all righteousness. Then he suffered him. And Jesus, when he was baptized, went up straightway out of the water: and , lo, the heavens were opened unto him, and he saw the Spirit of God descending like a dove, and lighting upon him: And lo a voice from heaven, saying, This is my beloved Son, in whom I am well pleased. (Matthew 3:13–17)

Why does Jesus come to John to be baptized? If the purpose of baptism is to have one's sins washed away, there seems to be no point in Christ, who is without sin, being baptized. This situation was clearly as perplexing to John as it is for most of us.

John, in fulfilling his ministry, has been preparing the way for the coming of Christ. When Jesus arrives, John, in great humility, acknowledges the Christ. Realizing his relationship to the Savior, a sinner to the one who has not sinned, John states that it is he who is in need of being cleansed. John asks Christ why He is coming to him. Christ answers in one sentence, "Suffer it to be so now: for thus it becometh us to fulfil all righteousness." In that sentence are volumes of answers, many of which are to questions we have probably failed to ask.

The central question is, "Why does Christ, who is without sin, need to be baptized?"

Christ's purpose on this earth is to atone for our sins and to show us the way. When we break down what transpired in the exchange between the Pharisees, Sadducees, and John, and the instructions Christ gives John, we have revealed to us why and what we must initially do to receive exaltation.

The admonition and exhortations John gives to the detractors of Christ establish the first principle of the gospel, faith. If they fail to believe in Jesus Christ, then all that follows by way of instruction and example is wasted upon them. If they have no faith, they will not repent. If they do not repent, the miracle of the effects of baptism will not be made available to them. If they are not baptized by water, they will not receive the baptism of the Holy Ghost. "He that believeth and is baptized shall be saved; but he that believeth not shall be damned" (Mark 16:16).

If these ordinances are not carried out, we will be damned. To be damned is to be held back as a dam prevents the flow of a stream. If we fail to choose and follow the stream prescribed by God that leads back to His presence, we will find ourselves damned, with no further spiritual progression.

Knowing we have found that it is often unwise to follow the teachings of mere mortals, Heavenly Father clarifies John's teachings: "Suffer it to be so now." It cannot be more plain that we are to do what God says, and do it now, whether or not we understand His reasoning. We are to have faith. We are to obey. In time, God's purposes for all things will be revealed.

Jesus needed to be baptized for several reasons. First, the rules for salvation apply even to Christ. Even He is not exempt from the rules God has deemed necessary for salvation and exaltation. Second, He was to demonstrate for us the proper method of baptism. Third, if Christ needed to be baptized and to obey all the rules, it should be blatantly obvious to us how great is our need for this saving ordinance. Fourth, baptism is an absolute necessity if we, and Christ, are to become righteous, "for it becometh us to fulfil all righteousness."

Christ said "us," meaning him, John, and everyone else. Christ said "all righteousness" because baptism is the first step in our growth and development toward achieving perfection. To fulfill all righteousness is to be perfect. We must always remember that achieving perfection is what we are instructed to do. Christ has told us to be perfect even as is God our Father.

When we truly come to understand that it was necessary for Jesus Christ Himself to be baptized and that He is giving us the perfect example of what we are to do and when we are to do it, we begin to realize the enormous necessity and importance of this saving ordinance. Baptism is the first step we must take in starting a new spiritual life in accordance with God's wishes.

Christ received His baptism prior to the start of His ministry. His baptism occurred prior to His forty-day fast. It occurred prior to the insulting temptations presented to Him by Satan. It occurred prior to His working of miracles, prior to His gathering of those who would become apostles, and prior to every other aspect of His ministry. There is no accident to the order in which the ordinations necessary for Christ's salvation, as well as our salvation, occur.

These first saving principles of the gospel, faith and repentance, are experienced as internal and emotional events that pave the way and prove to Heavenly Father, and ourselves, that we have sufficiently grown to a point where we are ready to perform the outwardly demonstrative ritual of baptism. We prove that we have had a change of heart through our faith and repentance. We demonstrate through the ritual of baptism that we are ready serve God and help establish His kingdom here on earth as it is in heaven. It is through baptism that we declare we have put off the natural man and willingly submit ourselves to God's law.

We become as children. We become humble, attentive, and not only willing but hungry to be taught. If you ask what it is we are to be taught, you are on the right track. It is simply this: We are to learn all things that pertain to exaltation.

Baptism is the first time that we covenant before God and witnesses that we give our life to Him. In humility, our sins are forgiven and forgotten. We are washed clean from all of our sins and our past transgressions. We give ourselves to God and His kingdom with all that entails. We covenant to do so for all time and eternity.

In our agreement, or covenant, with God, we agree to do what He commands, and He agrees to bless us. In our part of the baptismal covenant, we agree to stand as a witness of Christ at all times and in all places. We agree to obey all the commandments of God. We give our lives to Him. We are born again of the water and begin our life anew. We show our dependence on Heavenly Father and declare our humility to Him. We agree to be faithful to the end. We become teachable. We agree that the rest of our earthly endeavor will be in the service of Heavenly Father and the building up of His kingdom. We agree to love others as we love ourselves.

We will serve His children, our brothers and sisters, throughout the world. We will mourn with those who mourn and weep with those who weep. We will share in their joys and laughter. We will give a hand to those in need both spiritually and temporally. We will receive a hand when we sincerely need it. We will always remember Christ and His Atonement. We will love the Lord our God with all our heart, might, mind, and strength. We will no longer fit God into our life; rather we will mold our lives around His. This is our part of the agreement.

Heavenly Father's part of the covenant is to bless us. When we ponder just what these blessings may entail, they will be limited only by our imagination and our spiritual maturity. Initially, we receive the companionship of the Holy Ghost. As we grow in the gospel, once again line upon line and precept upon precept, the magnitude of His additional blessings will be revealed, and those blessings will grow exponentially.

To receive His blessings, we must remain humble. We can sit at the Master's knee. We become more deeply aware of proper temporal behavior and attitudes and more acutely aware of scriptural doctrine, instructions, and the mysteries of God's kingdom. We come to a greater love for life and our fellow man. We develop greater compassion for all that others are experiencing.

We do not give our children meat before they have teeth. God will not give us the blessings of the doctrinal meat of the mysteries of salvation and exaltation until we have sufficiently developed the spiritual capability to ruminate, digest, and receive value from the pearls of wisdom and knowledge that He would have us recognize. Also, revelations will not come forth unless we will use that information wisely to assist our fellow man and further develop God's kingdom.

God's blessings for us are innumerable. They will come in the form of temporal blessings and spiritual blessings. Our daily trials will not be lessened. Indeed, as we grow spiritually, they often increase. The blessings come in how we are able to handle those trials and problems. We realize the opportunity for growth and strength they afford us. Those trials, travails, and tribulations allow us to gain character and wisdom. They allow us to assist others who struggle with the same difficulties. They are a constant reminder of our dependence upon God. We will appreciate

His love, justice, and mercy. We will appreciate the Atonement of Christ. We will become better fathers and mothers, husbands and wives. We will become better teachers. We will have more peace in our hearts and greater compassion for our fellow man. We will feel more of the love God has for us, and we will love others more deeply. We will be blessed with much greater peace and comfort through the Holy Ghost. And this is just the beginning.

At some point in time, the mysteries of the heavens will begin to unfold before us. We will understand the creation of the heavens and earth and our role in the plan of salvation. We will be blessed with greater perfection in our lives. We will become enlightened. The mysteries of the fall of Adam and Eve will be appreciated for what actually transpired. We will understand the Exodus and the Flood in their entirety. We will understand the Atonement and all that it implies and does.

We will understand what transpired before Moses, Abraham, Malachi, John the Baptist, Peter, Paul, and John. The visions that the prophets have seen will become clear and be understood by us. We will be protected from the destroyer. We will come to be receivers of the Abrahamic covenant. We will know God and Jesus Christ and be able to rule and reign with them throughout all eternity

There is yet more concerning baptism that we need to examine: the symbolism pertaining to it.

To facilitate our spiritual education, God had provided us with many ways to learn from the scriptures. The Bible is replete with the principle of symbolism. This method of teaching allows us to receive truth and knowledge far beyond what a practically stated principle may convey. So it is with baptism. Far beyond the outward conveyance of our declaration to serve God and receive His forgiveness and cleansing of our sins, baptism is symbolic of Christ.

All things in the Bible lead to a witness of Christ, a witness that He is the Savior, a witness that He would in a future time die for us or that in past time He gave His life for us. The doctrines of salvation are a witness that He is Alpha and Omega, the beginning and the end. There is nothing in the Bible that does not lead us to ponder the central issue and claim, as well as the most important event that ever occurred or ever will occur.

Baptism is given to us as a symbolic representation of the death, burial, and resurrection of Jesus Christ. We must put off the natural man. Our old carnal life devoted to temporal ways is voluntarily given up. Our old self, through the exercise of our moral agency, dies. When we are baptized, we symbolically do what Christ did in reality. Our old self dies. As Christ was buried in the tomb, so we are buried in a watery grave. As He arose to be born again in immortality and eternal life, so we arise from the water to be born again in like manner. As He came up out of the water and received the Holy Ghost as His constant companion, so may we, in our newly cleansed state, receive the same gift by one who is a legally ordained administrator of God.

When Christ was resurrected, His body and spirit were reunited. He was then judged by God and given His birthright. When we come forth from the water and then receive the Holy Ghost, we are symbolically resurrected in similitude of Christ. Our future rewards are based upon the judgment we will receive based on the choices we make after baptism and throughout the rest of our life. Through obedience to the first and second principles of the gospel and then fulfilling the first and second gospel ordinances, which are baptism and receiving the Holy Ghost, we demonstrate our desire to follow God's commands. By remaining faithful to the end, we demonstrate the depth of our commitment. We prove our desire by our actions. We show our love by our works.

I would like to briefly readdress the issue of how we are to be baptized. I take a great risk at this juncture in offending those of various sects who have been baptized in a manner other the manner described here. I mean no offense. After coming to understand baptism as directed by the Lord, through the teachings of the Bible, I came to realize that I received, at the age of nine, only half a baptism and even that was invalid.

In addition to all the aforementioned aspects relating to the necessity, importance, and symbolism of baptism, we need frank clarity concerning this ordinance.

Remember that the ordinances, both temporal and spiritual, given to us by God are His laws and commandments. To fulfill His law, we must act exactly, completely, and correctly as instructed. Remember that we have been shown not only the why but the how by Christ. Here is a review of and addendum to the facts pertaining to baptism based on Christ's perfect example.

Baptism is a requirement for exaltation. Christ, who was to become exalted, showed us it was a necessary requirement for Him. If He needed to be baptized, so do we.

The word *baptism* is derived from the Latin and Greek root *baptisma,* which means "immersion." Christ's death cannot be symbolized by burial in water unless we go under the water. Christ was immersed, as evidenced by His coming "straightway out of the water," as noted in Matthew 3:16. Also, John always searched for enough water that would allow him to perform this ordinance. "And John also was baptizing in Ænon near to Salim, because there was much water there: and they came, and were baptized" (John 3:23).

For baptism to be complete, we must receive the Holy Ghost by a legal administrator. Christ received the Holy Ghost from God our Father, who then exclaimed, "This is my beloved Son, in whom I am well pleased" (Matthew 3:17).

John's authority was limited to baptism. We would do well to note that the dove has always been a sign of peace, comfort, truth, and innocence. In the case of John, the dove was a sign of confirmation that he had truly baptized Christ. The Holy Ghost does not take on the shape or form of a dove or any other animal. The dove in the case of Christ's baptism was symbolic. The Holy Ghost is a personage of spirit just like Heavenly Father and Christ. It is power, protection, influence, peace, comfort, and truth that we receive from the Holy Ghost.

All ordinances must be performed under the hands of a legal administrator. A legal administrator is commissioned of God. He has the priesthood conferred upon him by one already holding the priesthood. The powers, rights, and authority of the priesthood are his as long as he is living a worthy life in accordance with God's laws, the laws of the land, and the laws and ordinances pertaining to the church as established by Jesus Christ. A priesthood holder is one in a priesthood line of authority that reaches back to Jesus Christ and His apostles.

Some people believe that a belief in Christ is all that is necessary to be saved. Acts 16:29–33 notes:

> Then he called for a light, and sprang in, and came trembling, and fell down before Paul and Silas, and brought them out, and said, Sirs, what must I do to be saved? And they said, Believe on the Lord Jesus Christ, and thou shalt be saved, and thy house. And they spake unto him the word of the Lord, and to all that were in his house. And he took them the same hour of the night, and washed their stripes; and was baptized, he and all his, straightway.

This account of the conversion of the prison guard and the instructions given by Paul and Silas, as recorded by Luke, is a most interesting example of the subtleties conveyed in the scriptures. The jailer asks what he must do to be saved. The reply is to believe on Christ, and he and his household will be saved. This assumes, of course, that those of his house have sufficient desire and belief. However, contrary to most people's initial impression upon reading verse 31, none are saved at this point in time. They must first receive instruction pertaining to the gospel ordinances. They must have faith and a repentant heart. Paul and Silas instruct him and all his house in the principles and ordinances of the gospel. They teach them the plan of salvation. They are instructed in the covenants they will make. They are taught of the Holy Ghost and the straight and narrow path. Paul and Silas, with full knowledge of the gospel plan, teach all of the necessary elements prerequisite to baptism.

In his humility, with broken heart and contrite spirit, the jailer tends to the wounds they received during their incarceration. Then, and only then, after having been interviewed, instructed, and having repented of their sins, were these newly enlightened souls baptized. This is a stellar example that belief in Christ alone is not enough to bring about our salvation.

Yet being born again of the water is still only half a baptism. We must receive the Holy Ghost through a legal administrator. God the Father, having authority in all things, conferred the Holy Ghost upon Jesus Christ, as well as His priesthoods and all things appertaining to them.

Christ then ordained His apostles with the priesthood, which is the authority to do the work of God here on earth and to do so in the name of Christ. They in turn confirmed and ordained worthy members of Christ's church with the same powers, rights, and authority, and so established a legally authorized line of priesthood authority. This line continues today through The Church of Jesus Christ of Latter-day Saints.

Referring back to the second ordinance of the gospel, receiving the Holy Ghost under the hands of a legal administrator, no man takes this honor, meaning the bestowal of any holy gift, ordinance, or office, unto himself unless he has been called of God. No matter how good and righteous we are, no matter how kind and loving we act, no matter how deeply we feel the burning desire within our heart to serve God and our fellow man, we cannot exercise priesthood power and authority unless we have satisfied all the requirements necessary that authorize us to do so. We cannot receive this authority simply through personal study or by receiving a college degree.

These courses of action can be quite instructive, and much good can be gleaned from those pursuits. However, we must exercise discernment in the philosophies of man, especially when it comes to acting in the interests of God. Just because we feel called of God, it would be terribly arrogant of us to preach on our own without having satisfied the requirements established by the One he purports to serve. We must humble ourselves and follow the instructions of God, through Jesus Christ. It seems undeniably clear that God, in His perfection and house of order, would establish one way, and only one way, to rule and reign under His direction. In His perfect love, He will not authorize a multiplicity of interpretations of His laws and ordinances to be efficacious. His way is straight and narrow. The laws are set, the guidelines established. The example is given. The rules governing His house are plain, straightforward, and simple. There is no ambiguity. His authority is directly given to worthy individuals not taken upon oneself because of selfish desire. If we take this honor upon ourselves, no matter how righteous the intent, it is a selfish act. Selfish because there was no humility to follow the law as given by Heavenly Father. To be called of God is an honor given to us when we have acted in compliance with the requirements that allow membership in God's church. As we have seen, this begins with baptism and receiving the Holy Ghost.

When we then show ourselves worthy by honoring the baptismal covenants we have made, those who already hold the priesthood authority and its companion powers and rights may then confer that priesthood upon us. Likewise, a priesthood holder may then confer those powers, rights, and authority to another who has satisfied all the requisite principles and ordinances and issues of worthiness.

When a person is called of God, he is called by someone who has been authorized to act in God's behalf. "No man taketh this honour unto himself, but he that is called of God, as was Aaron" (Hebrews 5:4). Aaron was called of God, through a legal administrator, and was commissioned to act for Him through the Aaronic (Levitical) Priesthood.

Two encounters relating to baptism are recorded in Acts. Their importance lies is the fact that they are a paradigm for baptism, preaching the word of God correctly, receiving the Holy Ghost, and the manner and authority in which all this is to be done.

If we take the time to reflect that the apostles performed thousands of acts, we must conclude that only those of the greatest value for teaching and instruction in accordance with the will of God would be included in the scriptures.

Let us consider the instructions given to us in these chapters.

> And a certain Jew named Apollos, born at Alexandria, an eloquent man, *and* mighty in the scriptures, came to Ephesus. This man was instructed in the way of the Lord; and being fervent in the spirit, he spake and taught diligently the things of the Lord, *knowing only the baptism of John.* And he began to speak boldly in the synagogue: whom when Aquila and Priscilla had heard, they took him unto *them,* and expounded unto him the way of God more perfectly. And when he was disposed to pass into Achaia, the brethren wrote, exhorting the disciples to receive him: who, when he was come, helped them much which had believed through grace: For he mightily convinced the Jews, and that Publickly, shewing by the scriptures that Jesus was Christ. (Acts 18:24–28; emphasis added)

Here we find a man impassioned by the stirring of his soul at the good news of Jesus Christ. He knew of John's baptism, which was baptism by immersion. However, he was not aware that for baptism to be complete and efficacious, he also needed to receive the Holy Ghost as his constant companion. Nor did he know that the Holy Ghost must be conferred upon him by a legal administrator.

This man was eloquent enough to convince his fellow Jews that Jesus is truly the Christ. But we also find him, although well meaning and with good intentions, teaching incorrect principles. Emboldened with joy and enthusiasm at his spiritual transformation, he takes upon himself the authority to preach in the name of God.

This is a good man. This is the type of man the world always needs. Yes, he made a mistake. If left uncorrected after learning of his mistake, he would be guilty of excessive pride and a lack of humility, certainly not the traits a man called of God would cultivate.

However, upon meeting disciples endowed with the proper authority, he receives correct instructions and teachings regarding the plan of salvation. He receives a fulness of the gospel. Knowing the proper and correct principles of the gospel and receiving the authority to then teach them, he embarks upon the dwellings of fellow disciples to assist with their ministry.

In the following chapter, we have scriptural confirmation of four distinct facts having to do with baptism and the Holy Ghost:

And it came to pass, that, while Apollos was at Corinth, Paul having passed through the upper coasts came to Ephesus: and finding certain disciples, He said unto them, Have ye received the Holy Ghost since ye believed? And they said unto him, We have not so much as heard whether there be any Holy Ghost.

And he said unto them, Unto what then were ye baptized? And they said, Unto John's baptism. Then said Paul, John verily baptized with the baptism of repentance, saying unto the people, that they should believe on him which should come after him, that is, on Christ Jesus. When they heard this, they were baptized in the name of the Lord Jesus. And when Paul had laid his hands upon them, the Holy Ghost came on them; and they spake with tongues, and prophesied. And all the men were about twelve. (Acts 19:1–7)

In verse 2, Paul establishes through his questioning of the disciples that it is a necessary requirement to receive the gift of the Holy Ghost. When they reply that they have no knowledge of the Holy Ghost, Paul asks about their baptism, to which they reply "unto John's baptism." It appears that these disciples believed the principles of faith and repentance taught by John, but they had not received the first ordinance of the gospel in its entirety. They had not been baptized by immersion for the cleansing of their sins nor had they received the gift of the Holy Ghost.

Paul realizes that they are in agreement with the principles taught by John. They believe in Christ. But that is the extent of their conversion. Paul then goes on to explain to them the more perfect way, that along with belief they must perform required ordinances.

When the disciples are sufficiently instructed, they enter the waters of baptism. Having fulfilled that first necessary component of baptism, Paul lays his hands upon their heads and, through his priesthood authority, confers on them the second necessary component of baptism—receiving the gift of the Holy Ghost as a constant companion to lead and direct them. So powerful is their faith and belief that they immediately begin to preach the gospel to those around them in a language other than what is native to them. This is what it means to speak in tongues. These twelve had awakened within their souls one of their spiritual talents, and under the blessing of God and under the direction and power of the influence of the Holy Ghost, they preached and taught in a manner and with a power and authority they had never known.

The wonderful teachings of our Heavenly Father through the ministry of the Apostle Paul clarify these important facts:

1. We must have faith and then repent.

2. We must be baptized by one who is legally authorized of God.

3. Baptism consists of two components: immersion and receiving the gift of the Holy Ghost. This is baptism by water and fire and comprises two distinct acts.

4. We receive the Holy Ghost by the laying on of hands by a legal administrator.

5. Baptism opens the doors to miraculous manifestations of the Holy Ghost.

It is only after baptism that the Holy Ghost may be conferred upon an individual to be a constant companion. The Holy Ghost will be there for a baptized believer, "at all times and in all places," as long as he is worthy to receive this blessing. The Holy Ghost is a special gift, a special blessing, given to those who have chosen to participate more fully in the gospel ordinances as prescribed by our Heavenly Father. Proper behavior is rewarded over impropriety, whether that reward is by us as parents to our children, or by God to us, His children. God always blesses and rewards the faithful followers of His plan.

It is important to note that blessings and rewards are not always manifest immediately or even in ways that we understand. Many times they are; many times they are not. Many blessings come only after this earth life has ended. But that matters not. What is important is that we realize and understand that good works are always rewarded and bad works incur their own reward. Our actions, or works, will determine what our Heavenly Father may bestow upon us. It is always our choice whether we are rewarded with blessings.

For those who choose to do no works, understand this: God cannot bless us if we do not place ourselves in a position to be blessed.

THE DICHOTOMY
OF HOW WE ARE SAVED

For by grace are ye saved through faith; and that not of yourselves:
it is the gift of God: Not of works, lest any man should boast.
—Ephesians 2:8

But wilt thou know, O vain man, that faith without works is dead?
—James 2:20

It is no wonder that with all the seemingly paradoxical statements that abound in the scriptures, there would be nearly as many explanations and interpretations for how we are saved as there are people who preach the word. Fortunately, God has provided one and only one way to be saved. His plan does not vary or include different proposals by well-intentioned people, based on their personal scriptural interpretation of what is necessary for salvation. God does not author confusion. If we use the reasoning power God gave us, coupled with the influence of the Holy Spirit of Truth, it is clear that He would have only one method of salvation. Heavenly Father has not hidden what we must do to be saved.

A thorough reading of the scriptures coupled with prayer and meditation will help us understand this most important gift of salvation. There are key elements we should engage in if we are to receive deeper spiritual understanding and greater scriptural knowledge. We must study, pray, ponder, and reflect upon the issue at hand.

It is essential we pray to know the truth of things. We have been promised in James 1:5–6: "If any of you lack wisdom, let him ask of God, that giveth to all men liberally, and upbraideth not; and it shall be given him. But let him ask in faith, nothing wavering. For he that wavereth is like a wave of the sea driven with the wind and tossed."

After a prayerful request comes the guidance of the Holy Ghost. The Holy Spirit will tell us when we have got it right. God will not keep secret the fulness of His doctrine of salvation.

It is vitally important that we have a complete understanding of all His doctrines. We cannot base an entire concept around a single verse in the Bible. It is because this has been done so often that so many have strayed from the directions God gave us, particularly concerning salvation.

Before we can examine how we are saved, we need to understand what it means to be saved.

When we ask the average person what it means to be saved, the usual response is "to go to heaven." When we ask, "What is heaven?" the usual response is, "Where God lives." When we ask, "What does God do in heaven?" the usual reply is silence followed by a hesitant, "Well, I don't know," or "I guess He . . ." The general reply to the question of "What do we do in heaven?" which should be of greatest concern to us, is, "I don't know."

Sometimes the reply to the question of salvation is answered more accurately by the statement that our sins and transgressions will be forgiven. But if we are saved and we continue to sin or transgress, which is most probable for all of us, do we have to be saved again? Is one act of repentance and our personal acceptance of Jesus as the Christ enough to last a lifetime? If not, must we be saved over and over again? If that is the case, why not just wait until right before death and ask for forgiveness and to be saved? That would certainly save a lot of time and effort.

Simply stated, to be saved is to overcome death. The key element, however, is that there are two deaths!

I picture a man quickly being swept downstream in a swollen river. Exhausted, unable to help himself, unable to even speak, he rushes toward certain death. From the bank, someone throws a life ring to the drowning man. Miraculously, the ring slides over his outstretched arms and cinches itself around his body. The drowning man is hauled ashore. When he has regained enough strength, he looks around for his savior but cannot see him.

Does he offer thanks to the person he owes his life to? Does he search out the man who saved him? Does he continue to do the things that led to him being consumed by the river, or does he take the path that leads away from danger? Does he allow his understanding of being saved to change his life for the better? Perhaps he does, and perhaps he does not.

Christ overcame those things that we were unable to overcome ourselves. He has thrown us a life ring. Because we are sinners, we could not overcome sin; because we are mortals, we could not overcome death. Christ was the first to do both. In doing for us what we are not able to do for ourselves, He has opened the door that leads to salvation that otherwise would remain forever locked.

Thus, having been given the opportunity to be saved, it is imperative to reconcile the issue of being saved by grace or being saved by works. To do that, we must understand death.

Death can be separated into two parts. The first is physical death; the second is spiritual death. The first is easy to deal with because it is so familiar to us. At a certain point in our mortal existence, our bodies wear out and cease to function. The temporal game is over, and we experience physical death.

The second, or spiritual death, is a much more interesting subject and one that, surprisingly, we are more familiar with than we realize. In Revelation 20:12–15, we read:

> And I saw the dead, small and great, stand before God: and the books were opened: and another book was opened, which is *the book* of life: and *the dead were judged* out of those things which were written in the books, *according to their works.* And the sea gave up the dead which were in it; and death and hell delivered up the dead which were in them: and *they were judged every man according to their works.* And death and hell were cast into the lake of fire. *This is the second death.* And whosoever was not found written in the book of life was cast into the lake of fire. (emphasis added)

Here we have revealed a key piece of the puzzle that helps unify salvation by grace versus salvation by works. A more thorough examination of this will follow in chapters fifteen through nineteen.

We also find in these few short scriptures a confirmation that there is a second death and a wonderful explanation of what it is. Simply stated, we will all be judged according to our works. If our works have not been satisfactory, we will be cast out from the presence of God. This second, spiritual death will burn in our hearts and minds and is compared to being cast into a lake of fire. Once again, we will conduct a more thorough examination of these principles in a later chapter. For now, it is enough to establish that there is a second death, that the second death is to be removed from God's presence, and that our works play a part in our salvation.

We had our first experience with this second death in the premortal existence. When one-third of our brothers and sisters chose to follow Lucifer and were cast out of heaven, they began a separation from the presence of God that will last for all eternity. When they chose not to keep their first estate, not only did they give up the privilege of obtaining a physical body, but they gave up one of the greatest blessings of all, the blessing of living with their brothers and sisters and Heavenly Father in a state of exaltation for the duration of eternity.

For those who kept their first estate, there are choices to make. If we are to avail ourselves of the atoning sacrifice of Jesus Christ and avert this second spiritual death and the terrible anguish of being separated from the presence of God, we must make correct choices. Of course, it follows that our choices affect our works, and our works affect our choices.

With the introduction of a second death, it would seem that salvation would become more complicated, especially with the considerations of being saved by grace versus salvation by works. Wonderfully, God has reconciled these seemingly confusing and complex issues in a most simple way.

But we need to cover one more event before we can lay to rest the dichotomy of salvation. At this precise point in Heavenly Father's plan, when all the forces of the past four thousand years had combined to confuse mankind about what they (and we) had to do to be saved, a most miraculous and divine event took place: the ministry and Atonement of Jesus Christ. The Atonement of Jesus Christ marks the meridian of time. However, the foundation for the Atonement was laid in the very beginning of time by our first parents, Adam and Eve.

How they exercised their agency would bless us forever.

chapter fifteen

THE FALL OF ADAM AND EVE AND THE ATONEMENT OF JESUS CHRIST

This is my commandment, That ye love one another, as I have loved you. Greater love hath no man than this, that a man lay down his life for his friends. Ye are my friends, if ye do whatsoever I command you.

—John 15:12–14

Christ laid down His life for us. We are His friends. We are commanded to do whatever He asks of us.

The greatest gift given, and the greatest event that has ever occurred or ever will occur throughout all eternity, is the atoning sacrifice of Jesus Christ. It is because of, and through, His Atonement that we have been freed from the first and second deaths.

Christ freely and voluntarily suffered a torturous death so that we would be able to share in His birthright. He suffered torment, abuse, and anguish to give us all that He is to receive. He gave His life so that death will have no claim on us.

If we can come to an understanding of the Atonement of Jesus Christ, what it truly means, why it was necessary, what it actually did, and its effects upon us, we will then understand these deaths and begin to understand the varied aspects of salvation. When we are enlightened with regard to salvation and our role in that process, it will be much easier for us to correctly exercise our agency in accordance with God's laws.

No event in eternity is as important as the Atonement. From beginning to end, the Bible testifies of the coming of Christ and His divinity. Lambs without blemish were sacrificed as a type of Him to come. Christ, the spotless one, was sacrificed for us. A lamb's blood was shed as a precursor to the lifeblood shed by our Savior. Moses, a type of Christ, led Israel to the promised land. Christ leads us to the promised lands of heaven.

All events from the premortal existence to the death of Christ have led to the Atonement. As the only perfect child of Heavenly Father, the only one who followed God's laws and precepts without fault while still a spirit child, Christ was the only one who could atone for us. He alone possessed the right and privilege and blessing of Heavenly Father to carry out the plan of salvation. He, and we, knew and agreed that He would be our Savior. At that premortal time, we knew the only thing that mattered in life was to overcome trials and temptations so that we could exercise proper choices in accordance with God's will. We knew that this life would be a testing ground to prove our devotion and love for Him and that we would have to begin that exercise by proving our faith.

All existence led to the Atonement of Christ. All life follows.

Before we can understand the Atonement, we must first know what it means. The meaning of *atone* is to make amends or reparation for a wrongdoing or a wrongdoer. Because we are sinners and transgressors and as such are not able to enter the kingdom of heaven, for Heavenly Father to make good on His promise that we may be joint-heirs with Christ, someone is required to make amends or repay the debt we cannot pay. This Christ did.

Many are familiar with the breakdown of the word *atonement*: at-one-ment. Viewed in this context, the purpose of the Atonement is to be one with God and Jesus Christ. To be a joint-heir, we must be one with Christ. To abide with Heavenly Father, we must be at one with Him. And we are "ment" to be one with both. To do so, we must repay the debt we owe.

And just what is this debt that is so far beyond our ability to pay? It is everything around us. It is our homes and property. It is the apartment we rent. It is the bridge some may sleep under. It is the dwelling place of the homeless as well as those more fortunate. It is the money provided to us to facilitate our circumstances. It is all the temporal blessings we have in our lives. It is our food and clothing, our cars and trucks. It is the land we are blessed to live in. It is this earth we live on. It is our wives and husbands and children. It is the opportunity to experience life in all its myriad complexities. It is all we have and all we have not.

God created this world where we have been blessed to live. He created the bodies our spirits have been blessed to inhabit. He has provided everything we need to live and progress. By law and rights, everything in creation is His. As for us, we have been given temporary stewardship over His possessions. We are to care for the land. We are to care for our families. We are to care for each other. We are to take care of ourselves. Our bodies are the temples of the Lord where His Holy Spirit may reside.

We are to listen to God and obey His commandments. We are to obey the prompting of the Holy Ghost. The degree that we fail to do what we are asked, within the limits of our capabilities, is the degree that we are unprofitable servants.

Only by achieving perfection can we repay Him fully and perfectly. And perfection is not available to us in this life, hence, the need for a Savior.

What magnificent love the Savior has for us! He took upon himself all our sins and transgressions. He made payment for all we were unable to pay. He made amends for our jealousies and petty squabbles, our anger and pride. He paid for our selfishness and parsimony with His life.

No matter how diligently we try, we are unprofitable servants and always in the Savior's debt. This is due to the simple fact that even when we do our very best to be humble, selfless servants, the blessings we receive from Heavenly Father far outweigh the good that we have done. We always receive more than what we give. And if we examine how many of His children do little or nothing that He has asked of them, the issue becomes clearer still. Even they are blessed mightily. Even those who work against Him are blessed. At the least, they are sustained during their mortal life. At the most, they have earthly treasures beyond measure

The love and mercy of our Savior is boundless and limitless. He will make up all our individual debts. Each of us has differences in what we are able and unable to do for ourselves. All He asks is that we do the best we can do. Will we sometimes fail? Of course. Will we sometimes move backwards? There is that possibility. Will we give of ourselves halfheartedly? On occasion. But no matter how badly we stumble, if we get back up and give it our best effort, He will always make up the difference.

I hope that it is clear why this is the greatest event that will ever occur. We will have the opportunity to not die in our sins, and we may live through Christ. Heaven's gates that would otherwise be locked to us for all time and eternity will swing open through the atoning sacrifice of our Lord and Savior. The kingdom of heaven may be ours.

But even though it may be clear why the Atonement is unparalleled, let us take a closer and most worthwhile look at what would have transpired if it had never taken place. And to do that, we need to go back to the time of Adam and Eve.

> But now is Christ risen from the dead, and become the first-fruits of them that slept. For since by man came death, by man

came also the resurrection of the dead. For as in Adam all die, even so in Christ shall all be made alive. But every man in his own order: Christ the firstfruits; afterward they that are Christ's at his coming. Then cometh the end, when he shall have delivered up the kingdom to God, even the Father; when he shall have put down all rule and all authority and power. For he must reign, till he hath put all enemies under his feet. The last enemy that shall be destroyed is death. (1 Corinthians 15:20–26)

What a clear and penetrating exposé of the Resurrection, the Fall, the Atonement, who belongs to Christ, that all glory is to be given to God and that the last enemy is death.

Now the first fruits are the earliest produce of the season. They are also the first products, results, or profits of any activity. Because we are unprofitable servants, we have eliminated any measure of being a first fruit. But Christ, in His divine glory, is profitable. He was the first of all Heavenly Father's children to rise from the grave. He was the first to overcome death in both its definitions. He is the product of perfection, the Son of the living God. He has produced results that enable all who will listen to receive exaltation and glory that they, being Christ's, might be given back to God our Father.

Might Christ be judged as profitable? A rhetorical question. He has given increase to Heavenly Father's kingdom that no one else could approach. Never seeking for selfish vainglory, He gives all to God, who in turn, promises to give all back to Him and to us, if we will only but allow Him to.

In the above quoted scriptures, we find in verse 22 a clarification of verse 21. Adam, and by inference Eve, ushered in physical death or what we know as mortality. "For since by man came death" refers to Adam. They were also the first to experience spiritual death. They were cast out of the garden and separated from the presence of God. They no longer had the constant presence of the Holy Spirit. They were then subject to the enticements and temptations of the devil. Only by adherence to the first principles and ordinances of the gospel was the gift of the Holy Ghost, which is the right and privilege to have as a constant companion based upon one's faithfulness, again given to them.

If Adam was the first man in mortality, and a legal and authorized administrator must confer these ordinances upon him, how was this done? We need simply to look back to the first principles of the gospel and go from there. Adam needed to first have faith in God and then repent of his transgression, even though the transgression was a justified act. Because there were no other mortals present, his baptism and gift of the Holy Ghost was conferred upon him under the hands of divinity. This act performed by a divine being set the precedent for further acts in kind and was repeated when Jesus received the Melchizedek Priesthood from Heavenly Father, as stated in Hebrews 5:6.

Some fourscore times in the Gospels, Jesus Christ referred to Himself as the Son of Man. Two examples are found in Matthew 16:27–28: "For the Son of man shall come in the glory of his Father with his angels; and then he shall reward every man according to his works. Verily I say unto you, There be some standing here, which shall not taste of death, till they see the Son of man coming in his kingdom."

In 1 Corinthians 15:21, we read, "By man came also the resurrection of the dead." Then, verse 22 puts the relationship of the acts of the man Adam and the man Jesus Christ in perspective: "For as in Adam all die, even so in Christ shall all be made alive."

I have repeated this scripture because of the paramount importance of one word. The word is *all*. Though all must suffer physical death due to the transgression of Adam, *all* will be resurrected through the love and grace of God. Every single person who has ever lived, is living, or ever will live will be resurrected. The bands of death brought about by the Fall are broken. Though we are all sinners we will all have life immortal. Christ did for us what we could not do ourselves. The manifestation of God's perfect love is shown by allowing His Son, Jesus Christ, to atone for our sins and suffer death.

No man has ever been asked to make a sacrifice to this degree, and none ever will. It is true that Abraham was asked to offer his son as a test of his, as well as his son's, faithfulness. Also, it was important that this act be recorded as a type of that to come. But his hand was stayed. The act was interrupted. Human sacrifice is not, will not, nor has ever been a part of God's plan.

In 1 Corinthians 15:23, we receive further clarification: "But every man in his own order: Christ the firstfruits; afterwards they that are Christ's at his coming." We are all Christ's. He redeemed us. He paid the price for us to be together. He was the first; we come after. He has shown us the way. He will continue to show us the way.

The Lord's Prayer, found in its entirety, is in Matthew 6:9–13. For added validation and clarity to the discussion of God's kingdom, we should examine verses 9–10 from that prayer: "Our Father which art in heaven, Hallowed be thy name. Thy kingdom come. Thy will be done in earth, as it is in heaven."

When we pray for His kingdom to come, we are praying for His will to be exercised here and now by us as individuals and collectively as a society. His will is that the laws and ordinances that define His heavenly kingdom will prevail here on earth. It is to this end that Christ came to earth and established His church. Christ ordained apostles, teachers, and others. He taught them correct principles in accordance with the scriptures. He opened their eyes to understanding. He clarified parables for those in positions of authority. He gave to some the power to seal divine ordinances here on earth so that they would be in effect in heaven. He commanded that the gospel be preached to everyone.

His established kingdom is growing today. Not all will abide by God's rules. Not all will obey His laws. There is at present a separating of those who believe and obey, and those who do not. Now is the time of the great separating of the wheat from the chaff. When all has been done and the inhabitants of this earth have aligned themselves with either Christ or Satan, then God's kingdom here on earth in all its glory will be delivered by Christ to our Father. Our Savior has sought no glory for Himself. His only desire is for that aspect of the plan of salvation to be fulfilled and all glory be given to His Father.

All the earthly individuals who are in positions of authority and who exercise that authority in defiance of God's will, and all those who knowingly acquiesce to that evil, will not be of the kingdom. They will have refused the reign of Christ. They will come forth in the resurrection of the unjust. They will not be counted as Christ's and are not His at His coming. They are enemies of righteousness and will be under His feet as the earth is under the heavens. The last enemy to be destroyed is spiritual death because physical death has been overcome for all. Those who inappropriately exercise their agency will be damned from the presence and influence of God and the Holy Ghost. They will suffer the second, or spiritual, death.

We are at present in the midst of establishing God's kingdom here on earth. The results of our choices are clearly defined above.

Understanding the reasons of a given set of circumstances goes a long way in helping us make a correct choice. If we go all the way back to the

Garden of Eden, we may gain valuable insight into understanding the Atonement and its effect in our lives.

The great fall of man! It is tragic to me that this event seems to be so misunderstood. Poor Eve is continually blamed for the turmoil and difficulty we face in this life. "If only she had not partaken of the forbidden fruit, we would be living in paradise." "Life would be so easy if only Eve hadn't given in to temptation." The erroneous accusations and incorrect inferences abound whenever sin and temptation are discussed. The truth of the matter is that if Eve had not partaken of the forbidden fruit, we would not be here today.

Adam and Eve were living in a paradisiacal state in the Garden of Eden. All things were prepared for them. All their needs were fulfilled. Food was plentiful and living conditions perfect. There was joy and happiness, and God was there to instruct them. One of their instructions was to be fruitful and multiply. Another was not to eat of the fruit of the tree of knowledge of good and evil.

> So God created man in his own image, in the image of God created he him; male and female created he them. And God blessed them, and God said unto them, be fruitful, and multiply, and replenish the earth, and subdue it: and have dominion over the fish of the sea, and over the fowl of the air, and over every living thing that moveth upon the earth. (Genesis 1:27–28)

In Genesis 2:16–17, we read:

> And the Lord God commanded the man, saying, Of every tree of the garden thou mayest freely eat: But of the tree of the knowledge of good and evil, thou shalt not eat of it: for in the day that thou eatest thereof thou shalt surely die.

In Genesis 3:1–7, we have the intervention of Lucifer, who is symbolized by the serpent.

> Now the serpent was more subtle than any beast of the field which the Lord God had made. And he said unto the woman, Yea, hath God said, Ye shall not eat of every tree of the garden?
>
> And the woman said unto the serpent, We may eat of the fruit of the trees of the garden: But of the fruit of the tree which is in the midst of the garden, God hath said, Ye shall not eat of it, neither shall ye touch it, lest ye die. And the serpent said unto the woman, Ye shall not surely die: For God doth know that in the day ye eat thereof, then your eyes shall be opened, and ye shall be as gods,

knowing good and evil. And when the woman saw that the tree
was good for food, and that it was pleasant to the eyes, and a tree
to be desired to make one wise, she took of the fruit thereof, and
did eat, and gave also unto her husband with her; and he did eat.

And the eyes of them both were opened, and they knew that
they were naked; and they sewed fig leaves together, and made
themselves aprons.

It is critically important at this juncture that we realize that God's
plans will not be thwarted. His plans, conceived in omniscience, cannot
fail. He will use any seemingly bad event or mishap to further His wishes.
Here the tables are turned on Lucifer.

We find Lucifer in a crafty and beguiling way questioning Eve in an
attempt to persuade her to eat of the forbidden fruit. His first deception
is by implying, through his question of what they are allowed to eat, that
they may eat of any of the fruit in the garden. Eve states that they are
commanded not to eat of the fruit of the tree of knowledge of good and
evil, for they will die. At this point, she is speaking of a physical death.

Lucifer, with truth gained from foreknowledge, spins the facts and
states that she will not die. He then attempts to invalidate God's love by
saying that He would not have us be as He is, that He would not have us
be wise, that He would not have us know good from evil and be as the
gods, that He would not have our eyes opened to the truth.

At this point, Eve is not aware of spiritual death because of the veil
of forgetfulness discussed in previous chapters. She believes that if they
are cast out of the garden they will suffer a mortal death. The great truth
revealed here is that there was no death in the state of paradise where
Adam and Eve found themselves. Eve knew that here they would live
forever, and there would be no mortality unless they were cast out of
paradise. Death for them did not exist in their present state.

But we also find Eve being blessed with a marvelous revelation. While
contemplating the choice before her, whether to live in innocence or
experience progression as the gods, she is prompted by the Holy Ghost
and realizes what must necessarily take place if she and Adam are to keep
another commandment they were given: to be fruitful and multiply. Eve
realized that birth must take place in mortality. In their state of innocence
and immortality, they were unable to keep that particular commandment.
To carry out God's instructions to be fruitful and multiply, Eve realized
the necessity of eating the forbidden fruit. There could be no other way

Adam, knowing of the actions of Eve, realized that if he were to keep the commandment to be fruitful and multiply, he too must eat.

Upon being cast out from the garden, wonderful and fantastic changes took place. The earth changed. It was no longer in a paradisiacal state. Where once the earth offered up her abundance, briars and thorns, thistles and weeds took their place. Man had to work to sustain life. Mortality was ushered in. Pain and comfort, heat and cold, joys and sorrows were experienced. Laughter was countered by sadness, health by sickness, life by death. Man's days on earth were now numbered. The second death was a reality. All of this was a blessing second only to the Atonement.

How terribly Eve must have suffered so that we would be provided the chance to have a physical body. Who among us would have the strength and courage to do what she did?

It is time to honor Mother Eve. She did what Adam would not do. She committed a transgression so that all may live. She thought not of herself but of us and Heavenly Father's plan. She opened herself to thousands of years of scorn, ridicule, jokes, and misunderstanding. She gave up a life of immortal ease to suffer and finally die so we could continue our spiritual progression. Does this not remind us of the Savior?

Just as Christ, based on His works and faithfulness in the premortal existence, was chosen to fulfill a particular part of God's plan for our salvation, so were Adam and Eve. They were of the most mighty and faithful and blessed to be the first here on earth. God would not choose an unworthy person to carry out this most critical event that opens the gate to the path that leads us back to Him. Only the most worthy couple would do.

The very thought of sin and death evokes a primal response in most of us. Intrinsically, these thoughts give way to our greatest fears, fears of the repercussions of sin and fear of the consequences of death. These two basic elements are the substantive issues addressed by the Atonement. Christ suffered the effects of sin so that we could at some point in eternity become sinless. He gave His life to be the first fruits of them that slept, and He opened the gate to resurrection, immortality, exaltation, and eternal life.

We know very little of God's eternal laws that allowed Christ to overcome sin and death, but we have sufficient knowledge for our needs. What we know is that Christ had overcome all obstacles, tests, trials, and temptations. His salvation was sure. When He achieved perfection, there was simply no place for imperfection to enter; thus all things (sin and death) were overcome. Because He was the first of Heavenly Father's children to attain this state, He offered to show us the way. He offered to carry us across what we couldn't cross ourselves: that awful gulf between heaven and hell. He faced death and sin and became a conquering hero. He has shown us the cause and how to fight the fight. The battleground was Gethsemane, and the spoil of war was the Atonement.

And it was all waged on our behalf.

The first part of the Atonement took place at the Mount of Olives in the Garden of Gethsemane. Luke 22:41 records that Christ admonished His disciples to pray that they would not enter into temptation, and then He removed Himself "about a stone's cast [throw]." It was during this prayer that Christ took upon Himself the sins of every mortal who would ever exist. He knelt in prayer asking Heavenly Father if it be His (God's) will that the agony of what was being and was going to be experienced might be taken from Him. But in complete humility and servitude, Christ petitioned for His Father's will to be accomplished. An angel of heaven appeared and strengthened Christ throughout His ordeal.

The depth of agony at taking upon Himself the sins of all the world's inhabitants was so great that Christ sweat "as it were great drops of blood falling down to the ground" (Luke 22:44). Let us try to put that agony, which is simply incomprehensible to man, in some sort of perspective.

Sin is often pleasurable at the time of commission, even when we realize that we are engaging in it. When we take responsibility for our sins of either commission or omission and undertake the process of repentance, the resulting emotional and physical effects of sinning and repentance are mental anguish and physical pain.

In the case of sin, mental anguish precedes the physical manifestation of pain. This pattern is never reversed. When people state that the pain comes first, they are simply unaware of why they are experiencing what they are experiencing. This is an obvious truth substantiated by the universal answer to the question, "Why do you feel like this?" or "Why are you crying?" which is generally, "I don't know!" If we would take but a moment to reflect at that time, the cause of the manifested and demonstrative emotion would unfold.

During the Atonement, Heavenly Father allowed Christ to experience the remorse and anguish associated with all the sins that could be experienced by all people past, present, and future. There was not an actual transference of every individual's pain (sin), but rather a personal experience that was congruent, or analogous, to everyone's pain. If an actual transference of pain and sin occurred, mankind would be sinless for a certain period of time, and that would have been accomplished without the exercise of our moral agency. Because the plan of salvation is based on allowing us to choose for ourselves, this would be contrary to God's will. Of course, the resulting mental and physical anguish of experiencing the effects of everyone's sins was something only Christ could endure.

The result of this first part of the Atonement was that Christ experienced the anguish and torment of every sin and transgression that could be committed or omitted. Only by experiencing the effects of what everyone else could possibly experience could Christ then be able to extend true compassion, mercy, understanding, and knowledge. Only then could Christ face us in judgment knowing what we have been through. Only then could we face Him during judgment and know that He knows what we have gone through. Only by the experience of what we have suffered can Christ judge fairly, truly, righteously, and justly. Only by knowing that Christ has suffered more than we have can we accept His judgment in true humility.

Left worn and spent from the trials of Gethsemane, Christ would endure one more act of selfless service for the benefit and salvation of all Heavenly Father's children. He would give His body, His pure and holy temple, to a public and physical torture. He would suffer jeers and taunts, temptations and mocking. He would have His dignity insulted and His body whipped and torn. His physical and emotional endurance would be pushed to the limits of His capacity.

As we examined in the discussion of sin, Christ, being perfect, had no place for the imperfection of sin to enter. We experience the pain and anguish related to our individual sins, but Christ suffered vicariously the pain and anguish of everyone and every associated sin, although he never committed them.

It is the same for death. Christ stood as a vicarious proxy for us and died perfectly. His physical pain was greater than anyone has experienced at any time. The experience of physical death, as well as that of sin, must be experienced by all. The physical demise of a body is simply a transition from one state to another. Christ was permitted this necessary experience, and we will be blessed likewise. Thankfully, we will never have to suffer as He did.

It is given that no unclean thing may live in the presence of our Heavenly Father. Once Christ was resurrected and His body and spirit reunited, He was ready to be judged. And being flawlessly clean, He was perfectly qualified to live in the presence of God in exaltation and eternal glory.

Christ overcame death, experienced resurrection, and received judgment. Only one who is perfect could show us the way. There would be no equivocation, ambiguity, or erroneous instructions as to how and what we were to do concerning death and what was to follow. Christ paved the way and opened the doors.

The Atonement is a universal gift, yet a most personal one for each of us. We need to have a personal relationship with the Savior and understand what the Atonement means in our life.

From the moment of our premortal birth to the instant of our body's death, when our spirit leaves our body to our subsequent resurrection, from judgment to consignment, everything in our immortal existence either led to the Atonement or will become what it is as a result of the Atonement.

The Atonement of Christ is the most efficacious blessing of love we can receive. Through it, all possibilities are opened to us. We have the opportunity to live with God, Christ, and our families for eternity in a state of perfection and glory. It is given to us to become as Christ and Heavenly Father. It is a gift beyond compare.

IMMORTALITY VS. EXALTATION

So when this corruptible shall have put on incorruption, and this mortal shall have put on immortality, then shall be brought to pass the saying that is written, death is swallowed up in victory.

—1 Corinthians 15:54

Some people are often confused as to the meaning of certain scriptural passages when specific words seem to be used interchangeably. The most notable examples of this are immortality, exaltation, and eternal life. The clarification of their meanings lies in knowing the actual definition of those words, the context in which they are used, coupled with the spiritual depth of understanding of the individual reading the scriptures. Misunderstanding is not wrong. Pointedly, different levels of understanding work in accordance with the will of God. The understanding of concepts is added upon little by little as we grow in knowledge and show responsibility in using the revelations given them.

The mysteries of the kingdom and the greater or deeper spiritual meanings contained in the scriptures are not revealed to us simply to satisfy curiosity. We must be responsible in using what we receive. Only when we prove or show that we are willing to use what God has revealed to us in a righteous manner and in accordance with His wishes will more be given. The Savior said, "Give not that which is holy unto the dogs, neither cast ye your pearls before swine, lest they trample them under their feet, and turn again and rend you" (Matthew 7:6).

This admonition was given to the disciples to underscore the importance of the knowledge they were blessed to receive. They were warned of the danger and persecution that could be brought against them by the unrighteous. That exhortation is salient today.

When we consider the admonition presented to us in sharing our personal revelations, how much more judicious must God be in giving those revelations to us in the first place.

To lay a foundation for the clarification of *immortality* versus *exaltation*, we need to start with definitions.

Immortality is defined as the quality or state of being immortal, specifically, endless existence.

Eternal is defined as without beginning or end, existing through all time, everlasting, timeless.

Exaltation is defined as an exalting or being exalted.

Exalt is defined as to raise on high, elevate, lift up, to raise in status, dignity, power, honor, wealth, and so forth.

Here we have keys that unlock the door to some of the mysteries of the kingdom. To be immortal or live eternally is simply to exist forever. Nothing is implied concerning the quality of a person's postmortal life. To be immortal and eternal is simply to be.

I do not wish to underplay or diminish this most important state. This state of being is exactly the blessing we receive through the Atonement of Christ. It is a magnificent gift. It is what will allow us to be resurrected. This is the free reward for keeping our first estate.

Everyone on earth will at some point be resurrected. We will all have a reuniting of our spirits and bodies. Those who followed Lucifer and were cast out of heaven, the one-third of the heavenly host, never received and will never receive a physical body. For them, there can be no resurrection.

If there were no Atonement made, we could never be resurrected, and thus, we would have been consigned after our mortal death to exist in immortality and eternally as spirits forever, being subject to the rule of Satan.

Fortunately for us, this is not the case. The blessings of exaltation may be ours. Let us return to the scriptures.

> The Spirit itself beareth witness with our spirit, that we are the children of God: And if children, then heirs; heirs of God, and joint-heirs with Christ; if so be that we suffer with him, that we may be also glorified together. (Romans 8:16–17)

> Now I say, That the heir, as long as he is a child, differeth nothing from a servant, though he be lord of all; but is under tutors and governors until the time appointed of the father. Even so we, when we were children, were in bondage under the elements of the world: But when the fulness of the time was come, God sent

forth his Son, made of a woman, made under the law, to redeem them that were under the law, that we might receive the adoption of sons. And because ye are sons, God hath sent forth the Spirit of his Son into your hearts, crying, Abba, Father. Wherefore thou art no more a servant, but a son; and if a son, then an heir of God through Christ. (Galatians 4:1–7)

The purpose of the Atonement is to provide a resurrection for all mankind and to provide the opportunity for all to live with God. We should note here that the resurrection is inextricably tied to our judgment. And although immortality and eternal life is a free gift, exaltation is a reward for the faithful. And to be faithful is to do more than believe.

A clear and beautiful example is recorded in Matthew 16:25–27:

For whosoever will save his life shall lose it: and whosoever will lose his life for my sake shall find it. For what is a man profited, if he shall gain the whole world, and lose his own soul? or what shall a man give in exchange for his soul? For the Son of man shall come in the glory of his Father with his angels; and *then he shall reward every man according to his works.* (emphasis added)

We have been given the free gift of immortality and eternal life through the atoning sacrifice of Christ our Savior. Now, in addition to those blessings, we read that we might earn a reward according to our works.

There is clearly and succinctly set before us the solution to the dichotomy concerning salvation by grace or salvation by works.

God has only one plan for our salvation. It follows, then, that if there is only one plan for salvation, in simplicity there can only be one way to be saved. Heavenly Father has kept things simple for us. He knew that there would be myriad interpretations of His instructions concerning salvation and the meaning of the scriptures.

So it is with the dichotomy of salvation.

We are instructed that salvation came through the way, the truth, and the life, as stated in John 14:6: "Jesus saith unto him, I am the way, the truth, and the life: no man cometh unto the Father, but by me."

His is the one and only salvation, a free gift to all of us who kept our first estate. For the righteous and the wicked, death was overcome for both, and the gift and blessing of immortality and eternal life is given to one and all.

It may seem unfair that those who of their own volition have wasted their lives by engaging in all manner of sin should receive the same blessing as those who lived a life in accordance with God's commandments.

How could God, when He has shown us not only what we must do but also how we must do it, and even given us His Only Begotten to show the way, possibly give to the wantonly unrighteous the same blessing as the righteous?

Simply because the blessing for keeping our first estate is the same for one and all. That blessing is immortality.

We might question, "But if everyone receives the same blessing whether they obey the commandments or not, is that fair? Why bother to keep the commandments at all? I thought God was supposed to be fair!"

The answer is that God, our Heavenly Father, *is* fair and would not give way to confusion or contradiction. He would not give us instructions and then ignore our obedience or lack of obedience to those instructions.

God is fair. He is righteous. He is merciful and just. And both mercy and justice will be given us in the degree they are individually warranted.

God gave us laws and commandments, and whenever a law is given, so is a consequence for not obeying that law. He is not only a God of mercy but also a God of justice. Justice must be served.

God will grant exaltation to those who live in obedience to the law. This is their reward. For those who chose not to obey the law, their punishment is simply to receive nothing more than eternal life.

Exaltation is to live forever in the presence of Heavenly Father and Jesus Christ. It is to be a joint-heir with Christ and receive all that the Father hath. It is to receive all His mercy, justice, power, dominion, righteousness, and glory.

The outcome of failing to obey God's law is a two-edged sword. True, the blessing granted is immortality or eternal life outside the realm of Satan. The punishment is eternal life not spent in the divine presence of Heavenly Father and Christ.

The information here revealed is staggering! It points out that there must needs be more than one residence for all who kept their first estate: one abode for those who failed to obey (living out of God's presence) and one for those who did obey (living within God's presence).

chapter seventeen

COMMANDMENTS FOR SALVATION

If ye love me, keep my commandments.

—John 14:15

To be faithful—and here is the difference and a key issue concerning salvation and exaltation—is to actively participate in establishing the kingdom of God here on earth by obedience to the commandments of Heavenly Father. The faithful are bound by an oath, realize their duty to God, and humbly acknowledge their obligation to Christ and our Father for the Atonement. To be faithful is to manifest faith through works.

To have faith is a marvelous trait and is the initial element needed to progress to exaltation. But it is not enough. To put faith alone in its proper perspective, we need only to read a simple, succinct, clear, and instructive scripture: "But wilt thou know, O vain man, that faith without works is dead?" (James 2:20).

There it is. It is not enough to simply believe. It is not enough to simply have faith. However, faith is the beginning. From faith all things spring.

Let us put faith in its proper perspective and read the admonition of James:

> What *doth it* profit, my brethren, though a man say he hath faith, and have not works? can faith save him? If a brother or sister be naked, and destitute of daily food, and one of you say unto them, Depart in peace, be *ye* warmed and filled; notwithstanding ye give them not those things which are needful to the body; what *doth it* profit? *Even so faith, if it hath not works, is dead, being alone.*
>
> Yea, a man may say, Thou hast faith, and I have works: shew me thy faith without thy works, and *I will shew thee my faith by my*

works. Thou believest that there is one God; thou doest well: the devils also believe, and tremble. But wilt thou know, O vain man, that *faith without works is dead?*

Was not Abraham our father justified by words, when he had offered Isaac his son upon the altar? Seest thou how faith wrought with his works, and by works was faith made perfect? And the scripture was fulfilled which saith, Abraham believed God, and it was imputed unto him for righteousness: and he was called the Friend of God.

Ye see then how that by works a man is justified, and not by faith only. Likewise also was not Rahab the harlot justified by works, when she had received the messengers, and had sent *them* out another way? *For as the body without the spirit is dead, so faith without works is dead also.* (James 2:14–26; emphasis added)

Verse 24 tells us that through our works, we are justified. This goes well with the discussion of mercy versus justice noted in the last chapter. We are given the blessing of immortality as a free gift to all. However, the greater gift of exaltation must be earned. That gift is a reward. Matthew 16:27 tells us that "he shall reward every man according to his works."

Lastly, to underscore the validity, importance, and necessity of faith being joined with works, James states three times in thirteen verses that faith without works is dead. I think we have been fairly warned.

But what are these works that we must do?

All commandments were summed up in Matthew 22:37, 39. The two great commandments are "Thou shalt love the Lord thy God with all thy heart, and with all thy soul, and with all thy mind. And, the second is like unto it, Thou shalt love thy neighbour as thy self."

To understand what we are to do next, we need only to look to the life of Christ. He was a servant. He spread the gospel. He taught disciples. He mourned with the sad and downtrodden and rejoiced when appropriate. He attended services of worship. He went among the poor and homeless, the sick and the needy. Through the power of the priesthood that He held, and subsequently conferred upon His apostles, He healed the sick and blessed those in need of blessing. He gave that priesthood power to His apostles that they, acting in righteousness, would have the same power as He and His Father. And He gave those same apostles the power to confer that priesthood upon other worthy individuals.

We are commanded to have faith. From that faith springs repentance and a desire to become closer to God. The first outward ordinance we engage in, and the one that begins our journey to exaltation, is baptism. The second is receiving the gift of the Holy Ghost under the hands of a legal administrator, following the example and method established by Christ our Savior.

Along with the commandments of faith, baptism, and receiving the gift of the Holy Ghost, we are to endure in righteousness unto the end, as did Christ. We attend our church meetings. We partake of the wonderful gift of repentance when necessary. We take the sacrament. We pay our tithes. We visit the sick and needy, the widows and fatherless. We mourn with those who mourn and comfort those who stand in need of comfort. We rejoice with those who rejoice. We love others as we love ourselves. We share the gospel whenever the occasion arises. We edify one another, that is to say, we instruct each other morally and spiritually. And, we love the Lord our God with all our heart, might, mind, and strength.

In other words, we serve. When we do something for one of God's children, we have performed that act unto Him.

Read the instructions given to the apostles in Matthew 28:19–20: "Go ye therefore, and teach all nations, baptizing them in the name of the Father, and of the Son, and of the Holy Ghost: teaching them to observe all things whatsoever I have commanded you: and, lo, I am with you alway, even unto the end of the world. Amen."

The commandment is given to the apostles to baptize us. We, conversely, are commanded to be baptized. All works we do after baptism are to be in accordance with the example set by Christ. If we are wise, our faith will grow, and we will become faithful. Faith without works is dead, and only the faithful will be given the reward for their works—exaltation in the presence of our Heavenly Father.

chapter eighteen

THE PROMISE
OF THE HEAVENS

It is not expedient for me doubtless to glory. I will come to visions and revelations of the Lord. I knew a man in Christ above fourteen years ago, (whether in the body, I cannot tell; or whether out of the body, I cannot tell: God knoweth;) such an one caught up to the third heaven.

—2 Corinthians 12:1–2

What a revealing, significant, and seemingly cryptic statement. The Apostle Paul, while journeying to the established churches and seeking to expound to them the more perfect way, speaks of the third heaven. The churches of that day, deprived of means of speedy communication, let unholy habits, doctrines, and teachings creep in that were not in accordance with those that Christ had instructed His disciples in when He founded His church. A great part of Paul's ministry was to correct the leaders, members, and converts who had fallen into error concerning the teachings of Christ.

Here we have, by way of admonition to the Saints at Corinth, a clarification of an issue that is horribly confused today—the eternal reward of heaven. To be sure, there is more than one heaven. Paul clearly states that there is a third heaven. Of course, it stands to reason that if there is a third heaven, there must be a second and a first heaven. It also follows that if heaven has a glory, then the first, second, and third heavens must have their own particular degrees of glory.

There must have been great confusion at the time Paul addressed those Saints. A humble man, he sought not to glorify himself but his Father in heaven. At the beginning of chapter 12, in Paul's address to those Saints, Paul shares a personal revelation concerning the reward that might come upon the faithful. Keep in mind that, where there is a great reward, there is also the implication and admonition of a lesser reward.

"There are also celestial bodies, and bodies terrestrial: but the glory of the celestial is one, and the glory of the terrestrial is another. There is one glory of the sun, and another glory of the moon, and another glory of the stars: for one star differeth from another star in glory" (1 Corinthians 15:40–41).

In these verses, Paul writes of the glory of the celestial body and the terrestrial body. He mentions three degrees of glory and compares them to the sun, moon, and stars. Simply stated, a resurrected being will rise with a body appropriate to its heavenly reward. We will have a celestial body befitting the third heaven, which is the highest reward. The glory of this heaven is compared to the glory of the sun. A terrestrial body befits the second heaven. This glory is compared to the glory of the moon. Paul does not mention the telestial body; however, the first heaven is reserved for those who merit that reward. That glory Paul likens to the glory of the stars.

This analogy of sun, moon, and stars is used because of the way we view the sky. The natural elements were such an integral aspect of the lives of people during this period of time that it was a common element, or tool, for teaching principles. Christ taught in parables often revolving around seasons, trees, fruit, wheat, orchards, and so forth. These were day-to-day items that those of His era would be familiar with. Today, few know the necessity of grafting the branch from a good fruit-bearing olive tree to a wild olive tree or how necessary it is to carefully prune a tree so that it will bear good and abundant fruit. Few people are familiar with wheat and chaff or the purpose of a refiner's fire. Indeed, the vast majority of Americans today can barely see the stars above the lights of the cities they inhabit.

But of what we can see of nature today, it is readily apparent from our point of view that the sun is brighter than the moon and the moon is brighter than the stars, hence the three degrees of brightness are linked to three degrees of glory.

The brightest most gloried reward is compared to the brightness of the sun and is reserved for those who strive for and lead a celestial life in accordance with the celestial law. This would be living in accordance with the commandments of God. The reward for these righteous individuals is the third heaven of which Paul writes. It is within this third degree of heaven that the blessings of the Abrahamic covenant will transpire. This is the heaven of God the Father and Jesus Christ.

The glory of the moon rewards those who live in accordance with the terrestrial law. They will inhabit the second degree of heaven.

The lesser glory of the stars and the first degree of heaven is reserved for those whose lives have been lived in a telestial manner.

The blessing of the three degrees of heaven is that we may live in such a manner as to warrant the greatest reward Heavenly Father may bestow upon us. The admonition is that we live in such a manner as to warrant the least of His blessings. There is a place and a reward prepared for all of us according to our works.

chapter nineteen

A FAIR AND JUST GOD: SALVATION FOR THOSE WHO DIE WITHOUT KNOWLEDGE OF HIS PLAN

At first blush, it seems that only a select few of God's children will receive His highest reward. For us to earn the blessing of exaltation, we must have faith, repent, be baptized by immersion under the hands of a legal administrator, receive the gift of the Holy Ghost by the laying on of hands, and live to the best of our ability in accordance with the celestial law as prescribed by our Heavenly Father.

A legal administrator is one who holds the priesthood. The priesthood is the power, right, and authority to act in the name of God here on earth. The priesthood is received and passed on by the laying on of hands. As God the Father conferred all the powers, rights, and authority of the Melchizedek Priesthood upon Christ (see Hebrews 5 and D&C 84), Jesus, in turn, conferred that authority upon the apostles Peter and James. Such authority, lost during the Apostasy, is efficacious today through The Church of Jesus Christ of Latter-day Saints.

So few who have ever lived have had this opportunity presented to them. Even today, there are cultures and tribes that have never heard of Christ or God, let alone what they must do to receive His greatest blessings. What is to become of them?

What of those who have been led astray by false religions and teachers? What of all the billions of people who died without ever hearing of God's plan for our salvation? So many of His children never had and never will have a chance during their lives to hear of what they must do to gain exaltation.

Again, the demands of justice seem impossible to satisfy.

However, if we refer back to the most basic attribute of God, that being the quality and manner of His love, He must provide a way for everyone to uphold His commandments. There could be no other way for a fair and just God.

In fact, He has promised us just that. "It is written in the prophets,

And they shall be all taught of God. Every man therefore that hath heard, and hath learned of the Father, cometh unto me" (John 6:45).

This verse in the midst of a magnificent chapter dealing with salvation can be easily overlooked. While it is true that immortality is a free gift to everyone, and that alone guarantees salvation in either the telestial or terrestrial kingdom, all of God's children will be taught of Him and His commandments pertaining to exaltation. That exaltation, as a reward for faithful adherence to the commandments, secures immortality and eternal life in the presence of God and Jesus Christ and habitation in the celestial kingdom, or as Paul states, the third heaven.

The answer to the question of exaltation for all who die without the opportunity to hear what was required of them was known throughout the antiquities. This issue is treated forthrightly in 1 Corinthians 15. Prior to his expounding on the various degrees of glory (verses 40–41), Paul teaches the Saints concerning the resurrection of Christ: that He rose from the dead, that there will be a resurrection for us, and that when the last enemy—death—was conquered, Christ placed Himself under subjection to God so that God may be all in all. In other words, so God and His teachings, doctrines, and commandments may be presented to everyone.

This beautiful, clarifying statement about the performance of the ordinances that were being carried on at that time allows exaltation for those who passed on without knowing or hearing the gospel doctrine. "Else what shall they do which are baptized for the dead, if the dead rise not at all? why are they then *baptized for the dead?*" (1 Corinthians 15:29; emphasis added).

Baptism for the dead was a practice engaged in after the resurrection of Christ. It is obvious that His appearances to the apostles after His ascension to Heavenly Father and His resurrection had a greater purpose than simply to validate His predicted fate. After fulfilling all righteousness here on earth, Christ made postmortal appearances for numerous reasons, not the least of which was to further instruct the apostles.

That they were instructed in the ordinance of baptism for the dead must necessarily have occurred for it was that particular ordinance, along with the resurrection, that Paul was once again clarifying for the Corinthian Saints. Also, that ordinance could not be performed prior to Christ's resurrection, the reason being that the gulf between spirit paradise and spirit prison would not be bridged until the visit of Christ.

Before we examine the actual ordinance of baptism for the dead, we must look again at the atoning sacrifice of Jesus Christ.

Because we were not able to overcome sin and death, Christ stood as a vicarious proxy for us. He did for us what we could not do. He was our stand-in. He took our place in a required setting and performed what was required of us on our behalf. As a result of that performance, we are then able to receive the blessings associated with what was done for us, if we so choose. In other words, by standing as a vicarious proxy for what we could not do, He has given us the opportunity to exercise our agency and accept or reject the effects of the Atonement.

Applying Christ's example of vicarious proxy to the ordinance of baptism for the dead, a way was provided for every single one of Heavenly Father's children to receive the required saving ordinances of the gospel. Christ instructed and ordained the apostles to vicariously do this work for the dead, and they were given the power to confer this authority to other worthy members of the Church. It is absolutely necessary that the living stand as a proxy for the dead.

The ordinances of baptism by immersion and receiving the gift of the Holy Ghost by the laying on of hands through a legal administrator is performed today by the living for the benefit of those who have passed on, through The Church of Jesus Christ of Latter-day Saints, just as it was anciently. A proxy is baptized for a deceased individual by an authorized servant of God. After being baptized, the proxy receives the Holy Ghost by another authorized priesthood holder. These necessary ordinances are not able to be performed in the spirit world and are done here on earth.

While the physical or temporal body rests in the grave, a person's living spirit has the opportunity in the spirit world to accept or reject the saving ordinances that have been performed.

Just as on earth, those in the spirit world continue with their right of agency, so they might choose freely and of their own volition to accept or reject the ordinations that were performed vicariously on their behalf.

A loving and just Heavenly Father must provide a way for His children to accomplish what He has asked of them. To think that those who died without knowledge of the gospel and its rules and ordinances would be forever lost to the blessings of exaltation through no fault of their own is to deny the mercy of God. But to think that by virtue of that same circumstance, they would be absolved of what God requires for the rest of His children would be to deny His justice.

It is through the example of Christ that we have been given the example of vicarious proxy. Once again, mercy tempers justice and the demands of justice are fulfilled.

What a beautiful and simple plan. Nothing changes between the living and the dead: not the ordinances, how they are performed, or to whom they pertain.

SECTION V:

DEATH, THE SPIRIT WORLD, AND LIFE AFTER DEATH

chapter twenty

DEATH EXPLAINED

O death, where is thy sting? O grave, where is thy victory?
—1 Corinthians 15:55

One definition of death is the permanent ending of all life functions in a person. If this were true, how sad this short period of existence we spend on earth would be. With nothing to look forward to, this life would be a meaningless exercise in acquisition and loss, turmoil and strife, and the never-ending anxiety that what is contained in this existence is never enough. If death were the end of all life, there would be no use for morals or social mores, laws or regulations. Life with the imminent aspect of annihilation would be undertaken with the sedulously hedonistic creed, "Let us eat and drink; for tomorrow we die" (1 Corinthians 15:32).

But there whispers in every soul that there is more, that there has to be something beyond this seemingly futile exercise in the pursuit of ever increasing wealth. There has to be more than simply the struggle to survive. There is an undercurrent of meaning, beauty, rightness, and a positive aspect to our existence. There is an eternal hope, somewhere, that resides in nearly every person. There is a measure of intrinsic knowledge that life does not end when the body ceases to function. There is a testimony from the Holy Ghost within us and some small remembrance from the past in all but the most hardened souls that at death, life is not over.

So what is death? To what does death give way? And why are we sometimes so afraid?

To answer the last question first, fear of death is simply nothing more than fear of the unknown. Entering any situation with little or no understanding of the outcome would scare anybody. That is a good thing. It causes us to be prudent and cautious. It is a mechanism to help ensure survival. Fear protects us from encounters that will cause physical and emotional damage. Fear is a safety net.

But being caught in a net traps us. We can go no further than the confines of that device. We never prepare for what is on the other side of that barrier. So we limit our progression because of a lack of knowledge and understanding.

To what does death give way? What do we get when we conquer our fear of death or even our fear of confronting what death is about? What would our Heavenly Father have us know about death?

He would have us know this: death gives way to life. It is nothing more than a door that leads to greater experience and blessings. It is a pause at the end of one journey and the opening step to the next.

Why should we be afraid? Every one of us has already experienced death in our lives. I am not talking about the death of a loved one. I am talking about the change from our premortal state to the mortal one we find ourselves in at the present.

We all died pertaining to our lives as children in the presence of God. We were ushered into mortality as a necessary step toward our salvation. We needed to suffer trials and tribulations so that we might develop character, humility, and faith in an unseen God. We simply needed to experience life while separated from His presence.

We died that we might live in mortality. Christ died so that we will live in immortality and, if we choose, exaltation.

So what is death? It is nothing more than the separation of our physical body and our spirit body. This death is the first, or physical, death.

What happens next is where is gets really interesting.

chapter twenty-one

THE SPIRIT WORLD

Of course, upon death, our bodies are secured by burial, and they rest until our resurrection. But what of our spirits? What are they actually like, and where do they go to await the Resurrection? What is the spirit world? Is the spirit world heaven, hell, or a state of limbo? What takes place there, if anything?

These and many other questions come to mind when we muse about life after death. How often we may have wished for answers when they lay right before us.

Our state of existence after death and prior to our resurrection is in the spirit world. This third and last state of preparation is where we reside until we receive our final consignment to one of the three degrees of heaven. The spirit world is a habitation of fabulous undertakings. It is the precursor to simple immortality or exaltation.

The spirit world can be a place of rest prior to our resurrection, or it can be a place of torment. Every person who has lived is awaiting his resurrection and is at present living in the spirit world.

If we understand what our spirit bodies are like, we will have a much clearer picture of the spirit world.

John 20:14–17 recounts the appearance of Jesus to Mary Magdalene. At first, she supposes Him to be a gardener. Then when He calls her by name, Mary turns and recognizes the Lord. She either reaches for Him or Christ perceives she will do so, and He admonishes her, "Touch me not; for I am not yet ascended to my Father" (v. 17).

Christ is resurrected. His physical body has been reunited with His spiritual body, proof that our forms will be as man and woman in the resurrection, as they now are in the flesh.

After Christ ascends to His Father, He appears to the disciples in His resurrected form and allows them to touch Him. At first, they are overcome with fear.

And as they thus spake, Jesus himself stood in the midst of them, and saith unto them, Peace be unto you. But they were terrified and affrighted, and supposed that they had seen a spirit. And he said unto them, Why are ye troubled? and why do thoughts arise in your hearts? Behold my hands and my feet, that it is I myself: handle me, and see; *for a spirit hath not flesh and bones, as ye see me have.* (Luke 24:36–39; emphasis added)

Later in this same chapter, we read that in the Resurrection we will also be able to eat and experience physical sensations; Christ gives the example by eating broiled fish and honeycomb. Christ also shows us the spiritual and physical transformation that will take place during our progression.

But what transpired between the time of Christ's death and resurrection?

Where Christ spent the three days prior to His resurrection is stated by Christ Himself as He hung between the two sinners on the day of His crucifixion, when He tells one of the men, "Today shalt thou be with me in paradise" (Luke 23:43).

Now common reason, if not definition, dictates that paradise is a place of rest and joy, peace and a lack of strife. Of all the wonderful places on earth that we may have visited, none can equal the pleasurable experience of paradise. The very name connotes a place of great beauty, happiness, and freedom.

The antithesis of paradise is prison or hell. We know there are spirits in prison, and we know that Christ went to paradise for a period of time. It then follows that the spirit world must necessarily be divided into two sections: a spirit prison and a spirit paradise. These two realms make up the spirit world. Let us look more closely.

From the greatest teacher whom ever lived, we are instructed, among other things, about the nature and character of the spirit world. We are told what type of person inhabits which realm of the spirit world. We are given insights into character, wants, and desires of these inhabitants. We are shown the awful pain and torment that accompanies the realization of our mistakes and what separation from Christ and God for all time and eternity would be like.

Although the parable of Lazarus is multifaceted, we will look solely at its relevance concerning the interim period between the first death and resurrection.

There was a certain beggar named Lazarus, which was laid at his gate full of sores, and desiring to be fed with the crumbs which fell from the rich man's table: moreover the dogs came and licked his sores. And it came to pass, that the beggar died, and was carried by the angels into Abraham's bosom: the rich man also died, and was buried;

And in hell he lift up his eyes, being in torments, and seeth Abraham afar off, and Lazarus in his bosom. And he cried and said, Father Abraham, have mercy on me, and send Lazarus, that he may dip the tip of his finger in water, and cool my tongue; for I am tormented in this flame.

But Abraham said, Son, remember that thou in thy lifetime receivedst thy good things: but now he is comforted, and thou art tormented. And beside all this, between us and you there is a great gulf fixed: so that they which would pass from hence to you cannot; neither can they pass to us, that would come from thence.

Then he said, I pray thee therefore, father, that thou wouldest send him to my father's house: for I have five brethren; that he may testify unto them, lest they also come into this place of torment. Abraham saith unto him, They have Moses and the prophets; let them hear them.

And he said, Nay, father Abraham: but if one went unto them from the dead, they will repent. And he said unto him, If they hear not Moses and the prophets, neither will they be persuaded, though one rose from the dead. (Luke 16:10–31)

Two points of explanation are necessary for clarification. Abraham's bosom denotes the place of habitation for the righteous dead. It is the realm of paradise in the spirit world. The flame of torment that besieges the rich man is a metaphor that alludes to the searing pain of one's conscience, just as are the metaphors of fire and brimstone.

In this parable, we are given a pitiful and lowly beggar with no possessions who depends upon the mercy of strangers to sustain his mortal life. He is reviled and despised. He is so poor that any treatment, let alone medical assistance for his wounds, are beyond his means, and without pride and in complete humility, he consents to the ministering of wandering dogs to clean his sores. The servants of the rich man throw crumbs outside his gate, and it is on this that the beggar survives. Surely the rich man is aware of what transpires outside his home, yet he offers no help. He feels it is beneath him to condescend to poor Lazarus.

Lazarus dies and finds himself in the realm of paradise in the spirit world. He is comforted from all the ills and evils that were heaped upon him during mortality. That he is righteous is evident from his initial postmortal reward.

Meanwhile, the rich man dies and is buried. In these two examples, Christ teaches that although the body is planted in the ground, the spirit is received in another realm. For the rich man, that realm is hell, or the spirit prison, a fitting justice for one who has it within his temporal capability to be of great service and yet chooses his own selfish interests.

Christ told His disciples that it would be easier for a rich man to pass through the eye of a needle than to enter the kingdom of heaven. What an example this is of that statement. The challenge of the rich is not that they have riches, it is how poorly they generally exercise their stewardship over their wealth. After all, everything belongs to God. He created everything and allows us to possess what we have. He only asks for a tithe, or ten percent of the increase of what we have, and that we use our wealth to build up His kingdom. We do that by service to our fellow man. Clearly, this rich man was sadly lacking in those efforts. He was a highly unprofitable servant.

In verse 26, we are told of the great gulf that separates the spirit prison from spirit paradise. No one can cross this gulf, not Lazarus to assist the rich man nor the rich man to enjoy the comforts of paradise. They are each confined to their separate regions.

The resurrection of our Lord and Savior Jesus Christ had a great impact on what would transpire in the spirit world. Prior to the resurrection, as evidenced in this parable, there was no mingling between the righteous and the wicked, but that would change with the Atonement of Christ.

It may appear that we know nothing about what transpired after the crucifixion of Christ and His resurrection, but that is not the case. A clear account of His actions and what took place in the spirit world (paradise) was given to His apostles and recorded by Paul.

The reasons for recounting the events after His mortal death may be delineated as follows:

1. It is given to us to know the mysteries of the kingdom. This is a necessary part of our education if we are to receive, as a joint-heir, all that the Father hath.

2. This information was needed by the apostles so that they might teach the correct principles to the disciples of Christ's church.

3. What transpired was a key and critical aspect of God's plan for our salvation.

4. What transpired would allow all of Heavenly Father's children to hear the gospel and understand what is required for exaltation.

5. It was required to fulfill Christ's statement for God to be "all in all."

6. It was necessary to recount those events and train His apostles in the correct way so that mercy and justice would be served.

For there to be a clear understanding of what took place after the death of Christ, we must clearly understand key elements and terms. When our mortal bodies cease to function, or die, our spirits are separated from our bodies. Our body goes into the ground, and our spirits move to the spirit world. Make no mistake about it: the spirit world is not heaven.

Our spirits reside in one of the realms of the spirit world, realms described as hell (prison) or paradise (which, as we will see, is also a form of prison, though much more pleasant) for a period of time. The spirit world is a place of either penitence or a place of rest from the cares of the world. Be that as it may, the spirit world is simply a way station until certain of God's elements of the plan of salvation are fulfilled. It is a place given for our habitation where we wait for our resurrection, followed by our judgment and consignment to one of the three degrees of heaven.

To think that we immediately go to heaven or hell upon our mortal death is quite a confused issue in the minds of many. Those who have a limited understanding of the scriptures propagate this belief of instantly attaining our final resting place. In one sense that notion is true, though only in a very limited measure. It is true in the sense that for the righteous, being relieved from the burdens of mortality is heaven, and for the wicked, the searing sense of guilt associated with a life of sin and transgressions will torment one as befitting hell. The spirit world gives way to these experiences. It also gives way, as we will see, to many others. Prior to our examination of Christ's mission in the spirit world, let us differentiate between that world and heaven.

Heaven is the residence of God our Heavenly Father. It is His supernal kingdom. It is from heaven that He rules and reigns. He directs from His home those whom He will to carry out His instructions.

The spirit world is not where God resides. His heavenly home is peopled with His spirit children who have yet to be born into mortality. It is peopled as well by resurrected beings whose spirits and bodies have been reunited in their perfect form.

With the definition, differentiation, and clarification between the spirit world and heaven, we can now get down to specifics. "For Christ also hath once suffered for sins, the just for the unjust, that he might bring us to God, being put to death in the flesh, but quickened by the Spirit: by which also he went and preached unto the spirits in prison; which sometime were disobedient, when once the longsuffering of God waited in the days of Noah, while the ark was a preparing" (1 Peter 3:18–21).

There is no equivocation here. There is no hidden meaning. There is no ambiguity. The prison Peter refers to in his clarifying epistle is the spirit world, or spirit prison. It is deemed a prison because there is no escape from this realm until the day of judgment and consignment to our eternal reward.

This Peter is the chief apostle of Christ. It is he who opened the gospel to the Gentiles. It is he who stood as the mortal head of Christ's church after the Savior's crucifixion. It was committed unto Peter to hold the keys of the priesthood, conferred upon him by Jesus Christ. Peter was to act under the direct supervision of God (Christ), by revelations given to him through the Holy Ghost (see Acts 1:2).

We know that the spirits referred to are not a euphemism for living souls, or prison a state of mortal confinement. The telling clarification is stated in verse 20. The spirits preached to by Christ were, though sinners by virtue of the fallen state of man, nevertheless righteous in obedience to His commandments to the best of their ability. These were all the righteous people who lived prior to the Great Flood in the days of Noah. By reason, we may include these were all the righteous who died prior to the Atonement of Christ. These people were long dead to the mortal world. They were waiting for the gospel of Christ from the lips of the Master Himself.

But why would Christ preach to the righteous in the spirit world?

Peter reveals the answer in his following chapter: "For for this cause was the gospel preached also to them that are dead, that they might be judged according to men in the flesh, but live according to God in the spirit" (1 Peter 4:6).

Christ came to fulfill all righteousness and to fulfill the law. He came to bless all of Heavenly Father's children, living and dead, with what was necessary for them to gain exaltation. His blessings extended beyond those few mortal souls directly affected by His earthly ministry to include everyone who would receive His good news: those of the past, present, and future.

The dead live in a realm where it is necessary for them to have a proxy to stand in and perform the ordinances of baptism, receiving the gift of the Holy Ghost, and so forth. These rules were laid down as law and as such could not be violated if exaltation were to be achieved. God had to provide a way.

Christ preached all the instruction necessary for exaltation, in its complete and pure form, to the righteous spirits in spirit paradise. It then became their calling, duty, and mission to take those teachings to the wicked in the spirit prison so that the spirits residing there might be taught correct principles and accept or reject the work that would be done for them on earth. This work, of course, is baptism for the dead, conferring the gift of the Holy Ghost and all other ordinances that pertain to exaltation.

This is a paradigm of a fair and just God. It is the quintessential manifestation of the law of justice being served, yet tempered by mercy. Agency abounds in the eternities. It is the basic plank in the platform of eternal life. The freedom to choose is given to all without limits of time or location.

This preaching of the gospel to every spirit child of our Heavenly Father fulfills the Messianic statement of Malachi: "Behold, I will send you Elijah the prophet before the coming of the great and dreadful day of the Lord: And he shall turn the heart of the fathers to the children, and the heart of the children to their fathers, lest I come and smite the earth with a curse" (Malachi 4:5–6).

There is significant meaning in these two verses beyond what is now being discussed, and we will discuss that later. For now, let's talk about turning the hearts of the fathers to the children and the hearts of the children to the fathers.

By the love manifested by those on earth for those in the spirit world, the saving graces of the Lord may be fulfilled in their entirety. Those on earth may do for the deceased what they are not able to do for themselves.

Remember the admonition of Paul in 1 Corinthians 15:29: "Else what shall they do which are baptized for the dead, if the dead rise not at all? why are they then baptized for the dead?"

As Christ taught the righteous in the spirit realm, the righteous then have the charge to preach to the wicked in that part of the spirit world noted as prison or hell.

The parable of Lazarus and the beggar pointedly establish a great gulf separating the righteous from the wicked and that no person can bridge that gulf. And until the righteous in the spirit world had been given divine authority from Christ during the three days of instruction and authorization, no person had.

Christ was the first to bridge that gulf. He had to be the first because He was the only one with the power, right, and authority to do so. He shows us the way not only in mortality but also during our postmortal life. Why would He stop instructing us upon His mortal death? After all, He overcame death in both its forms that we may live.

We on earth must turn our hearts to those who have passed on and serve them as Christ has served us. The righteous Saints in the spirit world must do the same. When we have served the least of one of His children, we have served Him.

chapter twenty-two

OUR RESURRECTION

For if we have been planted together in the likeness of his death,
we shall be also in the likeness of his resurrection.

—Romans 6:5

It has been established that at death, our bodies are buried in the ground, and our spirits are consigned for a time in the spirit world. There is a separation of these two elements that make up our mortal living soul.

As was shown to us by Christ, our bodies and spirits will once again be joined. This is the meaning of resurrection. Our resurrection is a necessity; without it we would be limited in our ability to progress. A resurrection is an absolute requirement for us to receive further light and knowledge.

"The likeness of his resurrection." What a perfect state in which to exist for all eternity. We remember that when Christ appeared to Mary Magdalene, He admonished her not to touch Him. He had not yet ascended to His Father in heaven. However, He *was* resurrected. Upon Christ's resurrection, He appeared in a closed room, to His apostles. At that point, Christ invited them to touch Him (see Luke 24:39). They could feel His body. That His body was in a more pure form is understood by His ability to seemingly break the laws of physics that govern our mortal existence. We can rest assured that no laws of physics were broken when Christ appeared as a resurrected being, nor was there any manifestation of magic. It is simply that a higher form of existence, that being a resurrected person, is subject to a higher set of physical laws.

Because our bodies and spirits will be reunited in the likeness of His resurrection, we may expect our resurrected bodies to be in the same form, not subject to the diseases and maladies that bring sickness and death. We will take the form of bodily perfection. That this must be so is verified by the premise that no unclean thing may enter the kingdom of heaven. Any sickness or blemish would be judged to be unclean. Thus we can look forward to a certain peace that comes from the release of the burdens imposed by our mortal bodies.

The Resurrection is much more than the reuniting of our spirits and bodies. It also encompasses time.

There are two distinct periods when the Resurrection will occur. Those two separate and distinct periods will be divided further still. When we come forth will be determined by the choices we have made during our second, or mortal, estate.

We are fortunate that so much concerning the Resurrection is contained in the Bible. Let us read this scripture with the reasoning power God has given us and the spirit of enlightenment He has promised us: "And have hope toward God, which they themselves also allow, that there shall be a resurrection of the dead, both of the just and unjust" (Acts 24:15).

A resurrection of the dead! Of both the just and the unjust! What a wonderful scripture. Contained within this verse are tremendous truths. Not only is there to be a resurrection, but it is to be for all. The Resurrection is universal. It is for every soul who has or ever will exist. The Resurrection is for the good and the bad, the righteous and the evil.

If we notice the deeper meaning, we realize that there are two resurrections, or that a resurrection will take place at different times: one for the just, and one for the unjust. Again, we have complete clarity. There are two meanings in this verse. All will be resurrected, and the resurrection of the just will be separate from the unjust. This is a paradigm of monumental consequences.

To add verity to the above example, Matthew 27:52–53 states: "And the graves were opened; and many bodies of the saints which slept arose, and came out of the graves after his resurrection, and went into the holy city, and appeared unto many."

After Christ's resurrection, the first of all people to be resurrected came forth from their graves. Thus was coined the term first resurrection. This resurrection was not universal at this time. It pertained to a few individuals. I say few because of the billions of souls who had passed on prior to this time.

Many Saints arose but not all. None of the unjust came forth at this time. Those who remain unjust throughout their lives in the spirit world will never wear the title of Saint. Thus it is given to reason that as resurrection is universal and only the just arose, there must needs be a resurrection for the unjust, or a second resurrection.

The varying degrees of righteousness lived by just people will necessitate varying times to come forth in the first resurrection. Just as there are different degrees of glory coinciding with the three degrees of heaven, so are there different time periods within the first and, by inference, second resurrections.

"That Christ should suffer, and that he should be the first that should rise from the dead, and should shew light unto the people, and to the Gentiles" (Acts 26:23).

In Acts 26, the Apostle Paul bears his testimony to King Agrippa. After briefly recounting the events that led to his conversion, Paul teaches the king and those with him. He teaches of the resurrection of Christ. He teaches that Christ is the first of all humanity to break the bands of death and to open the prison that houses our bodies: the grave.

In 1 Corinthians 15:20, Paul again teaches this most important event, when he states: "But now is Christ risen from the dead, and become the firstfruits of them that slept."

Christ is the first fruits of all mankind who died before Him. He broke the bands of death and bridged the gulf of the spirit world so that we may follow in His footsteps. We are to do what He has done.

Through this inspired documentation of what transpired between Paul and King Agrippa, and Paul's instructive exhortations to the Corinthians, we have numerous truths revealed.

The way Paul's teachings are structured and recorded is no accident. When Paul uses the word *and*, it is to underscore the importance of the statement that follows: *"And* that he should be the first that should rise from the dead, *and* should shew light unto the people," as well as *"and* become the firstfruits of them that slept."

We see this again when we refer back to Matthew 27:52–53: "And the graves were opened; and many bodies of the saints which slept arose, and came out of the graves after his resurrection, and went into the holy city, and appeared unto many" (emphasis added).

This *and* is a powerful word. Through its use, we are encouraged to examine and ruminate upon each subsequent statement. We are given the opportunity to come to the realization of how important each following statement is.

Christ instructed and clarified those key elements of God's plan for our salvation directly to His apostles. He gave them the commandment to then instruct us upon His death. They did so with great emphasis.

When we examine these scriptures, the eternal truths we are being taught cannot be more clear or explicit. Here are some of Christ's teachings regarding the Resurrection:

1. The first of all of God's children to be resurrected was Christ.

2. Christ will enlighten the rest of us as to this resurrection that we will experience.

3. The Resurrection has already begun for some of God's children and took place after Christ overcame death.

4. Just as we were created in the image of God, so our resurrected bodies are in the same image. Our resurrected bodies and spirits are living souls, in complete accordance with the example shown by the appearance of Christ to the apostles, Mary Magdalene, and others.

5. To verify the truth concerning the Resurrection and Christ's teachings, resurrected souls (those bodies that were witnessed rising out of their graves) appeared to many people in the city of Jerusalem.

A saint is not accorded that title by well-meaning religious individuals who take upon themselves a supposed authority to grant that sacred title. Saints were and are all the faithful followers of the gospel plan that was laid down from the premortal existence and throughout mortality. Saints were the faithful followers of Christ who lived in accordance with the commandments. They are those who were the members of the Church He established during His ministry and that was continued during the ministry of His Apostles. Saints are also those who, not having had the opportunity to hear God's plan in mortality or partake of the required sacred ordinances necessary for exaltation, have accepted that plan in the spirit world. They have accepted the ordinances performed by proxy here on earth for their benefit while in the spirit world.

This is substantiated in 1 Peter 4:6: "For for this cause was the gospel preached also to them that are dead, that they might be judged according to men in the flesh, but live according to God in the spirit."

To be a Saint is not an honor bestowed upon a select few according to rules established by man. To be a Saint is a blessing offered to all God's children if they will live according to His commandments to the best of their ability, partaking of those sacred rites and ordinances prescribed by our Father in heaven.

Remembering that justice is tempered by mercy, we see how this comes into play in the Resurrection.

Further wonderful statements by the Apostle John concerning our resurrection are given to us, along with those of Paul's. Emphasized again is the separation of the just and unjust, their reward and punishment, and the order of resurrection.

Let us examine the scriptures in greater detail concerning the resurrection. I've highlighted with italics key items about the Resurrection and added parenthetical explanations for clarification. However, as we read the following scriptures, note the depth of meaning that pertains not only to the resurrections but also to other gospel principles already discussed.

> And cast him [Satan] into the bottomless pit, and shut him up, and set a seal upon him, that he should deceive the nations no more, till the thousand years should be fulfilled [the Millennium, or thousand years when Christ rules on earth]: and after that he must be loosed a little season. And I saw thrones, and they sat upon them, and judgment was given unto them: and I saw the souls of them that were beheaded for the witness of Jesus, and for the word of God, and which had not worshipped the beast, neither his image, neither had received his mark upon their foreheads, or in their hands; and they lived and reigned with Christ a thousand years. But the rest of the dead lived not again until the thousand years were finished.
>
> This is the first resurrection [those spoken of in verse 4 who rule and reign with Christ during the Millennium]. Blessed and holy is he that hath part in the first resurrection [Saints are blessed and holy and come forth in the first resurrection. Those who come forth in the second resurrection are not holy or blessed to rule and reign with Christ]: on such the second death [separation from God and Jesus Christ] hath no power, but they shall be priests of God and of Christ, and shall reign with him a thousand years. And when the thousand years are expired, Satan shall be loosed out of his prison [At this time, Satan will once again have the power to tempt and lead astray until he is cast into outer darkness forever]. (Revelation 20:3–7)
>
> Verily, verily, I say unto you, The hour is coming, and now is, when *the dead shall hear the voice of the Son of God: and they that hear shall live* [the gospel taught to those in the spirit world affording them exaltation]. For as the Father hath life in himself; so hath he given to the son to have life in himself; and hath given

him authority to execute judgment also, because he is the Son of man. Marvel not at this: for the hour is coming, in the which all that are in the graves shall hear his voice, and shall come forth; *they that have done good, unto the resurrection of life; and they that have done evil, unto the resurrection of damnation.* (John 5:25–29; emphasis added)

But every man in his own order: Christ the firstfruits: afterward they that are Christ's at his coming. (1 Corinthians 15:23; emphasis added)

For the Lord himself shall descend from heaven with a shout, with the voice of the archangel, and with the trump of God: and *the dead in Christ shall rise first* [The dead in Christ are those righteous souls that have passed beyond mortality. They are those who strove to keep the commandments to the best of their ability and live in accordance with the dictates of God and within the parameters of His laws in effect at the time of their mortality]. *Then* we which are alive *and* remain shall be caught up together with them in the clouds, to meet the Lord in the air [the Saints who are alive when Christ comes to earth the second time]: and so shall we ever be with the Lord. (1 Thessalonians 4:16–17; emphasis)

We have been given testimony by Matthew, John, and Paul, and that in great detail, about the Resurrection. These Apostles were taught directly by Jesus Christ. Their subsequent teachings were designed to convert, instruct, admonish, and edify. Their aim was to bring people to Christ. Their message was of love and compassion.

Their message was also one of practical matters: they taught of the who, what, when, where, why, and how. Their instructions are for the past, present, and future. They are our escorts along the straight and narrow path that has been illuminated by our Lord and Savior, Jesus Christ.

JUDGMENT

And the word of the Lord came unto Zechariah, saying, Thus speaketh the Lord of hosts, saying, Execute true judgment, and shew mercy and compassions every man to his brother: And oppress not the widow, nor the fatherless, the stranger, nor the poor; and let none of you imagine evil against his brother in your heart. But they refused to hearken, and pulled away the shoulder, and stopped their ears, that they should not hear. Yea, they made their hearts as an adamant stone, lest they should hear the law, and the words which the Lord of hosts hath sent in his spirit by the former prophets: therefore came a great wrath from the Lord of hosts. Therefore it is come to pass, that as he cried, and they would not hear; so they cried, and I would not hear, saith the Lord of hosts.

—Zechariah 7:8–13

When considering this great and defining facet of God's plan for our salvation, our personal judgment, we should realize His preeminent desire is to reward us, not punish us. It is paramount that we overcome the common negative connotation of the word *judgment*. God in His complete love will judge us as leniently as possible. He will be as fair and just as the laws He created and follows will allow. He will hold His judgment to the side of compassion and mercy. He will go as far as He possibly can to reward us as greatly as He is able.

As loving parents, we can identify. We discipline or punish our children as little as we can get away with while still fulfilling our responsibility to guide them in the ways of temporal obedience and spiritual righteousness. If we err in judgment, hopefully, we err on the side of compassion and mercy and love.

God does not err. When He judges us, we can be assured that it will be with and to a degree of empathy and mercy that we have never known. Still, His judgment will be just, as will be our reward.

On our day of final judgment, standing at the bar, we will undergo an examination of our lives. Not only will we recount how our mortal days have been spent, but we will be reminded by record of those days. We should be aware that the Book of Life spoken of repeatedly in the

scriptures is the heavenly record of how we spent our days of mortal proba-
tion. This book is our reminder. It will all be there in black and white for
us to see. All the righteous and unrighteous acts we have committed are
recorded. The times when we have shown compassion and mercy will be
documented, as will the occasions when we have shown apathy and severity. It is from this book that we will be judged.

Is that not fair? Should not judgment take into consideration the
truth, the whole truth, and nothing but the truth? Perfection demands
it must be so. And, thankfully, contained in perfection is charity, or the
pure love of Christ.

Of the many issues that are resolved through the Atonement, the issue
of justice and mercy is treated in a most forthright yet sensitive and clear
manner. How can the demands of justice be reconciled with the gift of
mercy? Can the laws that govern our actions simply be erased by the love
of the Savior? Is it enough to simply say we believe in Christ and then put
forth no further effort to be Christlike and thus nullify the commandments of conduct? Would that not then cheat those who so diligently and
faithfully strive to obey all God's commandments? Where is the justice
for those who serve so righteously as opposed to those who are tepid,
at best, in their commitment to the ordinances and rules prescribed by
Heavenly Father? And yet, where is the mercy for those who cannot serve
as greatly as others?

A clear-cut example of mercy versus justice is found in the parable of
the ten virgins, which reads as follows:

> Then shall the kingdom of heaven be likened unto ten virgins,
> which took their lamps, and went forth to meet the bridegroom.
> And five of them were wise, and five were foolish. They that were
> foolish took their lamps, and took no oil with them: but the wise
> took oil in their vessels with their lamps.
>
> While the bridegroom tarried, they all slumbered and slept.
> And at midnight there was a cry made, Behold, the bridegroom
> cometh; go ye out to meet him. Then all those virgins arose, and
> trimmed their lamps. And the foolish said unto the wise, Give us
> of your oil; for our lamps are gone out. But the wise answered,
> saying, Not so; lest there be not enough for us and you: but go ye
> rather to them that sell, and buy for yourselves.
>
> And while they went to buy, the bridegroom came; and they
> that were ready went in with him to the marriage: and the door
> was shut. Afterward came also the other virgins, saying, Lord,

Lord, open to us. But he answered and said, Verily I say unto you, I know you not. Watch therefore, for ye know neither the day nor the hour wherein the Son of man cometh. (Matthew 25:1–13)

A close examination of this parable sheds light on the issue of justice and mercy.

Verse 1: The kingdom of God is likened unto virgins because it will only contain the pure and chaste. All who profess to be followers of Christ and servants of God should strive to be like him.

Verse 2: Today is the age of the separating of the wheat from the chaff. The five wise virgins are those who are prepared in all things to meet Christ at His coming.

Verse 3: The five foolish virgins gave the appearance of being prepared. But is seems that they were only living the letter of the law. They had not made that deep personal commitment that signifies a true spiritual change of heart.

Verse 4: The wise brought oil to replenish their store when it ran low. Now this oil that is spoken of is representative of much more than the outward appearance of righteousness. The oil is one's testimony. It is one's belief. It is one's commitment to the gospel. It is that which we fall back on in times of trial and difficulty. It is that truth which is gained little by little over years of effort and faithfulness.

Verse 5: The time of waiting for the Second Coming.

Verse 6: Who might make the cry announcing that the Savior is come? The prophets.

Verse 7: A lamp's wick is trimmed so that it might give forth its most pure and brilliant light. We would like to be at our best and most prepared when meeting Jesus.

Verse 8: Those who have not properly prepared themselves spiritually will seek aid and assistance from those who possess a deep personal testimony and have lived the covenants they have made with the Lord.

Verse 9: The foolish are informed that they cannot be given assistance. They had wasted the time given to them to prepare. Further assistance at this appointed time would not be possible.

When Christ comes, we are to leave our beds unmade, come down from our rooftops, leave our fields and others behind, and come to Christ. We cannot give away personal preparedness. We cannot give away the blessings received from a lifetime of service and attention to the details of the gospel. We must earn a personal testimony, which requires time.

There was ample time for the foolish to study, pray, and ponder—time enough to ask the wise concerning their testimony and receive strength and assistance from them. But to do so now would place the wise in a position of not coming when beckoned. And, most important of all, this testimony and these experiences come from a relationship with God and cannot be had from another individual.

Verse 10: Christ comes and receives those who are prepared: those who are not still searching for what they previously should have acquired.

How is mercy served? The five wise virgins, in spite of their sins and transgressions, had done their best to follow the teachings of Christ and commandments of Heavenly Father. Because they served with sincerity and dedication as well as possible *within the limits of personal capability,* the atoning sacrifice of Christ the Lord made up the difference for what they could not do. He paid the price they were unable to pay, and they did the best they could. The mercy of the Lord was granted unto those faithful virgins and entrance into the kingdom was gained.

How is justice served? To allow the five foolish virgins entrance into the kingdom of God would be an affront to those who served so righteously. We reap what we sow. Those virgins who were slothful, no matter how righteous they appeared or how greatly they obeyed the letter of the law, lacked the spiritual commitment to guide the way they lived. They paid lip service to the commandments, and their actions were at best shallow. At the worst, they displayed an artificial righteousness.

To allow them into the kingdom would rob the wise virgins of the rewards their integrity and hard work had bought. And, it would unjustly reward the undeserving, making God's laws a mockery.

To further reconcile judgment and mercy, read Deuteronomy 11:1: "Therefore thou shalt love the Lord thy God, and keep his charge, and his statutes, and his judgments, and his commandments, alway." We must serve as diligently as possible, yet the mercy of Christ's Atonement will make up our deficits. We must realize judgment is a personal issue based on many factors.

We will all be held to the same standards so that there can be no favoritism. Our Master has no teacher's pet. It is because of this innate need for one standard of judgment that only one set of rules necessary for exaltation was given; only one person, Jesus Christ, is as an example; only one church, established by Christ, has all authority and complete truth; and only one law, God's law, is provided.

It is imperative that we realize that just as justice will be tempered by mercy, so mercy cannot be granted unjustly.

> And Enoch also, the seventh from Adam, prophesied of these, saying, Behold, the Lord cometh with ten thousands of his saints, to execute judgment upon all, and to convince all that are ungodly among them of all their ungodly deeds which they have ungodly committed, and of all their hard speeches which ungodly sinners have spoken against him.
>
> These are murmurers, complainers, walking after their own lusts; and their mouth speaketh great swelling words, having men's persons in admiration because of advantage. But, beloved, remember ye the words which were spoken before of the apostles of our Lord Jesus Christ; How that they told you there should be mockers in the last time, who should walk after their own ungodly lusts. These be they who separate themselves, sensual, having not the Spirit. But ye, beloved, building up yourselves on your most holy faith, praying in the Holy Ghost, keep yourselves in the love of God, looking for the mercy of our Lord Jesus Christ unto eternal life. (Jude 1:14-21)

When we look around us in a nonjudgmental way and notice how different lives are led, we notice a great discrepancy in adherence to the laws of God. That some people have advantages not available to others is obvious. What some people do with those advantages or fail to do with those advantages is often apparent. The manner in which some disadvantaged people live their lives is laudable and exemplary.

Some people delight in sin, and others abhor it. Some welcome sin, and others fight it with all their might. Some people endeavor to keep the commandments at all costs, and others only obey when it is convenient. Some people serve others while some prey on others. Some people profess a faith and belief in Christ and His teachings yet deny Him by their actions. Some believe they may delay the act of repentance until their dying hour and still be saved. Others do not profess that belief yet will do it anyway.

There are those in this life who know all of God's rules and requirements for exaltation. Within that segment of the populace some choose to obey those rules and others do not.

The point of all this is that just as there are countless numbers of people, there are countless degrees of righteousness, and it is upon the degree of individual righteousness we exhibit that we will be judged and our reward earned and given.

Almost all of us have been raised to believe in heaven and hell. Most of us believe we will spend eternity in either of those places. For the most part, that is true.

However, some people have a feeling there is a fundamental unfairness when an individual who lives a very unrighteous life is given the same eternal reward just because he believes in Christ as an individual who lives in accordance with the doctrines of God. People ask where is the justice? They question that if the eternal reward is the same, then why not "live it up" while in mortality and have the best of both worlds?

In other words, if by simply believing in Christ the reward is the same, regardless of how we live our life, why not sin, have fun, and live the easy life instead of struggling to adhere to a higher set of moral values as established by God's commandments?

These are good questions, and they deserve a good answer.

It would be unfair if justice and the reward were the same regardless of one's actions. If people could pick and choose what, when, and where they felt like obeying the commandments and to what degree and still receive the same blessings as those who diligently serve, that would indeed be a travesty of justice.

God will not let this happen. Let us get a little perspective on this issue. Suppose you have four children, each with his or her own room, and their rooms are their personal areas of responsibility. Just as our lives are sometimes messy and require attention, so do their rooms. So you make a covenant with them. This is the agreement.

"Kids, this is my house. I designed it and had it built under my direction by someone I trust. Now, I love this house, and I love you. I let you live here. You are my joy and my responsibility. But I hate a dirty house, and your rooms range from so-so to filthy.

"I've got a month's vacation coming up, so here's the deal. I have no desire to punish you, but for you to understand a reward, you must understand a punishment. You have to be able to compare the two. That doesn't mean you have to actually get punished, you just have to realize that if you choose not to obey me, you will get punished. On the other hand, if you do choose to obey me, I'll give you a reward. And I want you to realize that I want to reward each of you as much as I can.

"Okay. There are four things I want each of you to do in your rooms. Each task will have either a reward or a punishment attached. First: Pick up your clothes and toys off the floor and put them where they belong.

Second: Vacuum and dust your room. Third: Wash the windows in your room. Fourth: Help each other clean your rooms.

"Also, I want you to do these things in that order. I know the best way to accomplish these tasks, and I want you to learn the proper and correct way too. And I want it done by tomorrow. There is a time limit.

"Now, if you choose not to do the first one, you have to be punished. You won't be able to come on our family vacation. You will have to stay with mean Uncle Lucifer while the rest of us are having fun. I can't give you any reward for not obeying me, and I can't visit you while I'm on vacation either.

"If you do the first and second things I requested but not the others, you get to stay with Aunt Suzy. You like her and always have a lot of fun with her, but she lives far away from where I will be, and I can't visit you while I'm gone.

"If you do the first, second, and third things, you get to go to Aunt Annie's. She's the greatest. She's got all sorts of things to do, and she's lots of fun. And she lives close enough that I can visit you, so you don't get too homesick.

"Now, if you do everything I ask you—as best as you can—because I know you younger ones can't quite do everything just the way I would like it, but if you try the best you can on all four things, then we will spend the whole month at Disney World. We'll do all the rides and everything. Eat all the hot dogs and stuff we want. We'll go to the beach and ride the boats. We'll snorkel and sunbathe and go to movies and swim in the pool and ride horses and everything else there is to do.

"So you see, your reward or punishment is really up to you. Anything from Uncle Lucifer to Disney World."

This is a simplistic assessment and explanation of Heavenly Father's system of reward and punishment, but it does follow the plan.

We are saved by the mercy of God through the atoning sacrifice of Jesus Christ. This guarantees our reward in one of the three degrees of heaven. Our works will not get us into heaven. To be able to go heaven is an opportunity provided through the mercy of God. However, it is our works that will place us in either the first, second, or third heaven of which Paul teaches.

Various degrees of righteousness warrant various degrees of blessings.

To the degree that we obey God's laws and keep the commandments dictates the degree of heaven with which we will be rewarded.

Heavenly Father would have us all return and live with Him. But justice and fairness require us to put forth the effort. It truly is up to us what our reward will be.

The classic biblical example of this is the separating of the wheat from the chaff. Chaff is the waste product. It is scattered to the winds and removed from the presence of the wheat. It spends its eternal vacation with mean Uncle Lucifer or Aunt Suzy. That which is of value, the wheat, remains. But even wheat is not all the same. It is graded as to its value. Will it be profitable or not? To what degree will it be profitable? Will it be an asset or will it spoil?

We are all unprofitable servants but only because we can never repay Heavenly Father in full for what He has given us. However, we all can repay Him in some measure. Will some of us repay Him more than others? Certainly. Will some of us be of more value to Him than others? Of course. Will our Father reward in greater measure those of His children who obey His will than those who do not? The answer is a resounding yes.

However, we must remember that He loves us all the same, with the same depth and the same degree. God values all His children equally. He plays no favorites. Still, the responsibility rests on us. Whatever profitability and value He receives from us is that which we place on ourselves and is determined by our service to Him through our works.

In Exodus 18, Jethro gives counsel to his son-in-law Moses. From the morning to the evening, the Israelites line up for Moses to settle their disputes and pass judgment on various issues. The counsel he received from his father-in-law was to delegate authority and responsibility. It is in this same manner that our judgment will be conducted.

Writings in the New Testament are particularly clear as to the delegation of authority and by whom we will be judged. He has given the power, authority, and rights of the actual judging to another.

This sacred honor of sitting in judgment is outlined in John 5:22, 28–29, which states: "For the Father judgeth no man, but hath committed all judgment unto the Son: . . . Marvel not at this: for the hour is coming, in which all that are in the graves shall hear his voice. And shall come forth; they that have done good, unto the resurrection of life; and they that have done evil unto the resurrection of damnation."

The right and responsibility to judge is part of Christ's inheritance. Remembering that we may be joint-heirs with Christ, judgment should, at some point in the eternities, rest upon us. We can see this in the following scriptures, where Christ is speaking to His apostles: "And *Jesus said unto them,* Verily I say unto you, That ye which have followed me, in the regeneration when the Son of man shall sit in the throne of his glory, ye *also shall sit upon twelve thrones, judging the twelve tribes of Israel"* (Matthew 19:28; emphasis added).

"Ye are they which have continued with me in my temptations. And *I appoint unto you a kingdom, as my Father hath appointed unto me;* that ye may eat and drink at my table in my kingdom, *and sit on thrones judging the twelve tribes of Israel"* (Luke 22:28–30; emphasis added).

Previously I used Moses as an example for more than the obvious point of delegation of authority. Moses is a type of Jesus Christ. He led the Israelite nation to the promised land, a precursor to Christ leading us to the promise of exaltation in heaven. Moses showed his people where they could go and the best way to get there. He gave them God's law. He nurtured them and loved them. His delegation of authority was recorded to establish a gospel principle that has been ordained throughout the eternities.

This principle was again emphasized by Christ. Through His authority, His apostles were instructed as to what their judgment duties would entail.

> Dare any of you, having a matter against another, go to law before the unjust, and not before the saints? *Do ye not know that the saints shall judge the world?* And if the world shall be judged by you, are ye unworthy to judge the smallest matters? *Know ye not that we shall judge angels?* how much more things that pertain to this life? (1 Corinthians 6:1–3; emphasis added)

Once again admonishing the members of Christ's church at Corinth, Paul instructs the Saints to settle matters between themselves. He also reminds and instructs them of their future responsibility, that they will judge the world and angels. That same charge will fall upon those whose lives merit exaltation in the celestial kingdom.

What an honor and blessing to one day be deemed worthy enough to sit in righteous judgment, to be able to sit at the table of Jesus Christ in His kingdom. The precept is set before us in mortality and, subsequently, for the eternities. "For unto whomsoever much is given, of him shall be much required" (Luke 12:48).

And when our lives are over and we are judged on how we

completed the requirements we were commanded to fulfill, we will finally come to our reward.

OUR REWARD

For the Son of man shall come in the glory of his Father with his
angels; and then he shall reward every man according to his works.

—Matthew 16:27

To be consigned to a single heaven or hell is simply too general an eternal abode. Too many people live their lives in too many different ways. There are those who conduct themselves poorly and those who live abominably. There are those who live good and decent lives and those whose lives are exemplary. The rewards of eternity must comply with the variety of ways that people lead their lives and the circumstances into which they were born. Those who never had the chance while in mortality to learn what was expected from them by their Father in heaven will have that opportunity given to them in the spirit world. It is then that they will be held accountable for the choice they make concerning the saving ordinances performed in their behalf.

So we ask, what are these different levels of reward? Who will receive which reward? What takes place in each kingdom?

This is where we enter the realm of the three degrees of glory, or the three heavens talked about by the Apostle Paul.

The ultimate reward, celestial glory, is to live in the brightness of God's glory with Christ and the exalted Saints, and the ultimate punishment is living in the prison of outer darkness with Satan and the sons of perdition.

Satan's name is synonymous with perdition, which is the loss of all hope for salvation. It is utter ruin and damnation. Satan's minions became his "sons" or the sons of perdition. In the mortal realm, anyone who has gained a perfect knowledge of God and Christ and the Holy Ghost and then actively works to destroy the belief others have in those beings also become sons of perdition or angels to Satan. They have denied the Holy Ghost, Christ, and our Heavenly Father and have voluntarily joined with the devil to wage war against the Saints and God's plan. The everlasting anguish of hell through habitation in outer darkness is reserved for them.

Very few individuals who have gained this sure knowledge will act contrary to God's will. An example that we are all familiar with is Abel's brother Cain. One of the earliest recorded events given to future generations for their eternal instruction and warning was the story of Cain and Abel. Genesis 4 records their story. In verse 7, the Lord speaks to Cain and tells him that Satan desires him, and if he falls prey to Satan's desires, he (Cain) will eventually rule over him. Cain knows that the only place he will rule over Satan is when mortality is ended, judgment is passed, and Satan is banished to outer darkness. Only then, when consigned to a kingdom, will Cain rule the devil. Because Satan is the prince of darkness and the king and ruler of Evil during mortality, Cain will still be subject to Satan. The roles will be reversed following the end of mortality. This is a fitting punishment for both and a chilling warning for Cain. Yet Cain yielded to temptation and committed the unpardonable sin.

Paul's epistle to the Hebrews gives clarification to this unpardonable sin as well as the degree of enlightenment we must have to be guilty of committing the sin. In these verses, Paul is speaking to the Saints about the spirit world and heavens to come, with the admonition about what will transpire if they commit the sin against the Holy Ghost.

> Therefore *leaving the principles of the doctrine of Christ, let us go on unto perfection;* not laying again *the foundation of repentance* from dead works, and *of faith* toward God. Of the doctrine of *baptisms*, and of *laying on of hands, and of resurrection of the dead,* and of eternal judgment. And this will we do, if God permit. For *it is impossible for those who were once enlightened,* and have tasted of the heavenly gift, and were made *partakers of the Holy Ghost,* and have tasted the good word of God, and the powers of the world to come, if they shall fall away, *to renew them again unto repentance; seeing they crucify to themselves the Son of God afresh, and put him to an open shame.* (Hebrews 6:1–6; emphasis added)

This position is clarified further in chapter 10: "But we are not of them who draw back unto perdition; but of them that believe to the saving of the soul" (v. 39).

Apostles Matthew and Mark also talk about the unpardonable sin.

> Wherefore I say unto you, All manner of sin and blasphemy shall be forgiven unto men: but the blasphemy against the Holy Ghost shall not be forgiven unto men. And whosoever speaketh a word against the Son of man, it shall be forgiven him: but whosoever speaketh against the Holy Ghost, it shall not be forgiven him, neither in this world, neither in the world to come. (Matthew 12:31–32)

> Verily I say unto you, All sins shall be forgiven unto the sons of men, and blasphemies wherewithsoever they shall blaspheme: but he that shall blaspheme against the Holy Ghost hath never forgiveness, but is in danger of eternal damnation: because they said, He hath an unclean spirit. (Mark 3:28–30)

There is no sin so great as the sin against the Holy Ghost. To sin thus is to actively work against the kingdom of God and deny the light of Christ, which we have all been blessed to receive. It is to deny any and all spiritual enlightenment we have been given. It is to deny the truth that God lives, that Jesus is the Christ, and that the Holy Ghost exists. It is to deny the efficacy of the Atonement.

When I was a young boy on vacation with my parents, we stopped at the Oregon caves. These caverns stretch deep underground. They are cold and dark and beautiful, with stalactites and stalagmites, low ceilings and dripping water, cavernous rooms crossed by pathways and ladders leading up and down to more adventures lying just around the corner. My imagination conjured up visions of pirates and hidden treasure. I was an explorer discovering new worlds. I was Tom Sawyer and Huck Finn, and I held Becky by the hand. Injun Joe was behind us, and my bravery would save the day. It was a realm of magic and wonder for a boy who was still several years away from being a teenager.

And it was a nightmare for a claustrophobic mother.

At one point on the tour, several groups were gathered in a huge room and scattered among various locations. The ceiling was high, and there seemed to be a great distance between the walls of that section of the cavern. It was at this time that a demonstration took place. All the fixed lighting and flashlights went out. There was complete, total, and utter darkness. There were also screams, nervous laughter, and a general din of noise and consternation. The darkness was so pervasive that I could not see my hand held two inches in front of my eyes. We could not move, nor did we dare.

We were trapped immobile and at the mercy of our thoughts.

And then a single match was lit. That tiny light illuminated the entire cavern.

The sighs and sounds of relief were more than audible. You could feel the great oppression of the darkness being lifted. I could feel spirits being lifted as well.

Then the lights came on, and the tour continued with more sights being seen and appreciated. But the most remembered experience for my mother, my father, and me, as well as probably almost everyone there, was the experience of darkness for a moment and the feeling of helplessness. Our entire state of existence was frozen in one position for as long as the darkness lasted.

Fortunately we were surrounded by good people and caring guides. How terrible the experience would have been if we were left alone to fend for ourselves!

Now think of what outer darkness must be like. Imagine experiencing eternity in the complete and total darkness as only found in the most sequestered regions of the universe. Imagine spending all eternity living the second death, being forever cast away from the presence of the Savior, never having the light of Christ or the comfort of the Holy Spirit with you. Imagine being continually assaulted and assailed by Cain and Satan and their angels of darkness. Imagine existing where there is nothing to reference time, nothing to see. What would it be like to be all alone, a spirit, seeing nothing, being alone with only your thoughts, realizing that you once had the opportunity to receive some degree of heavenly glory? Think of the sounds of weeping and wailing and the gnashing of teeth. Imagine how your mind would sear with sadness and regret, hopelessness and despair. Think of an existence where your mental anguish burns for all eternity like a lake of fire and brimstone.

This is what lies in wait for those who have once had the light of Christ and then commit the unpardonable sin. This is the true and final hell.

"Rejoice, and be exceeding glad: for great is your reward in heaven" (Matthew 5:12).

This is more than a scripture of encouragement. It is a commandment. This is the charge given to us by our Heavenly Father. We are to rejoice. We are to look forward with anticipation to the wonderful blessings of heaven that await us. We have kept our first estate and will be duly rewarded. Great will be our reward. It will be of such magnitude that our mortal minds do not have the capacity to appreciate its measure.

Do not be too concerned with the aforementioned discussion of the unpardonable sin. To reach the depths of spirituality required before we could commit that sin is territory so remote that for the vast majority of use, we need not include ourselves in the company of the rare few who have explored that realm. Rest assured, very few people in history have received a sure testimony of God, Christ, and the Holy Ghost. Of those who have been so wonderfully blessed to receive that witness, a minuscule few have or will commit the unpardonable sin.

When we consider the rest of mankind, those excluded from the rare company of people with sure testimonies, it is almost beyond our ability to comprehend the depth of God's mercy being bestowed upon us. It may even initially anger some to hear that even people who have committed the most horrendous acts will receive a reward in heaven, simply because they kept their first estate.

The least valiant of Heavenly Father's children are those who love a lie. They are the people we find in present society who are carnal and sensual. They live their lives at the expense of others. They are selfish and shortsighted. They are murderers and robbers, thieves and criminals. They are the ones who refuse to be enlightened by the Holy Spirit. They may profess a belief in God and Christ, but their actions are contrary to the commandments. They neither change their ways nor repent, or if they do repent, it is insincere and holds no effect. True repentance leads to a change in behavior.

These people are the burden of society. Because of their actions, we are governed by civil laws, instituted by nations to define moral and ethical behavior. These people flaunt their rebellion of social mores and revel in illegal acts. They are the recalcitrant. This becomes their lifestyle, the course of their daily lives.

But rewarded they will be, by virtue of the fact that they made the initial choice to follow God's plan. Having failed to live in harmony with the will of God during mortal existence and then rejecting the plan along with its saving ordinances, they will still be blessed with a degree of heaven. And they will be comfortable there. They will continue in the same sociality that they chose to congregate with in mortality and then in the spirit world. It is true that birds of a feather flock together.

Their judgment and reward will be just. They will spend eternity in the least of Heavenly Father's kingdoms. They lived a base, carnal, and telestial life and will inherit the least or lowest heavenly reward—the reward of the telestial kingdom. Their glory will shine only as the stars. They forfeit all contact with divinity and will forever remember what could have been theirs. They will for the most part be somewhat happy. But they will be damned. They will have no further progression. They will never advance to the next highest kingdom with its greater rewards and glory. They will never see God or Christ. They will never be in the company of their righteous brothers and sisters. And the promise of the Abrahamic covenant will not extend to them. They will have no increase in the eternities. Such is the glory and reward of the telestial kingdom and those for whom it was intended.

We all know individuals that we would term "good." Jim is a good man, and Jane is a good woman. They are kind and considerate. They assist their neighbors, love their children, obey the laws of the land, and pay their taxes. They are loving and caring people. They travel through this life with a belief in God and may even go to church on occasion. They are helpful and kind.

Jim and Jane represent the great majority of Heavenly Father's children. They are concerned about leaving the world a better place for their children and grandchildren.

It is these people Jesus speaks to in His Sermon on the Mount. His admonition to them is to be doers of the word and to teach the word. However, to teach the word of God truly, we must live the word to the best of our ability. This means to follow and support the commandments of God, to partake of all the saving principles and ordinances, and to help others do the same.

These people are the salt of the earth, though the exhortation follows in Matthew 5:13: "But if the salt have lost his savour, wherewith shall it be salted? it is thenceforth good for nothing, but to be cast out, and to be trodden under foot of men."

These good brothers and sisters, the Jims and Janes of the world, have paid attention to at least some portion of the light of Christ that was made available to them. We have all been given, deep within our souls, the light of Christ. The extent that we acknowledge, develop, and share that light determines our eternal reward. Remember too that those attributes may be developed in the spirit world as well, but we have been counseled not to hide our light under a bushel. Once receiving that divine gift and the guidance and testimony of the Holy Spirit, we are not to turn our back on it. If we do, it will stand to our condemnation.

The great majority of the human race falls into the category of Jim and Jane. They are decent people. They have love and compassion and are thoughtful of others. They have a portion of the light of Christ; however, they fail to fully commit to living the stated decree that is necessary for exaltation. They do not fully repent, and they fail to receive baptism and the gift of the Holy Ghost under the hands of an authorized representative of Christ. They choose to live a good life but do not humble themselves to all the commandments of God. They choose how and to what degree they will serve Him. In other words, they are dictating the terms as to how and to what extent they will serve God and their fellow man. They fit the gospel around their lives and in accordance with what they choose to believe.

For these good people is reserved the reward of the terrestrial kingdom. The glory of this kingdom will shine as the moon. A kingdom of immensely greater blessings and reward than that of the telestial kingdom, it does not shine with its own light. Its light is reflected from those on high. And as with the telestial kingdom, the blessings of eternal increase have no efficacy. Though living in wonderful splendor and having lived respectable lives, they will be damned as to further progression.

The blessings of the Abrahamic covenant are reserved for those who inherit the celestial kingdom. Through that covenant, those who earn this reward will enjoy a posterity as innumerable as the sands of the seas or the stars in the sky. Their increase is eternal and everlasting. They will have the eternal joy and blessings that can only be received through bringing forth children. They will experience the deepest and most pure love that can be had.

All the prophets throughout the ages who have had the celestial kingdom revealed to them have been commanded not to record what they have seen. Of the many reasons, one is simply the incomprehensible nature of the third degree of heaven. This is the home of God our Father, Jesus Christ, and the Holy Ghost. Its splendor is of such great magnitude that it is beyond our grasp to fathom. We are limited in our reasoning and understanding, and to conceive of what that world is like is beyond our ability. We could not place the glory of the celestial kingdom into the parameters of our experience so that it would make any sense.

Such is the reward for those who live in accordance with laws of God. Those who avail themselves of the gospel principles and ordinances and endure righteously and faithfully unto the end will receive an incomprehensible reward.

The kingdom of God, the celestial kingdom, is a habitation of perfection. Within the walls of this heavenly reward are contained perfect love, perfect understanding, perfect joy and happiness. All who have soiled the premortal and mortal existence for God and mankind will be forbidden entrance, unless they repent with a broken heart and a contrite spirit. No unclean thing may enter the kingdom of heaven, an abode for the pure in heart, the humble and penitent. It is home for those who became as little children in the eyes of our Heavenly Father. It is the residence of those who served the Lord God with all their heart, might, mind, and strength.

Do those who inherit the celestial kingdom serve perfectly while on earth? No, they do not. They sin and transgress. But they repent and serve to the best of their ability. Of course, some serve more valiantly than others, but that is not germane in God's eyes. It is not how greatly we serve in comparison to each other but how we serve in comparison to our own ability or capacity to serve. We have all been given different talents and abilities. God knows this and allows for this.

In God's plan for our happiness, our service and commitment can be likened to a one-hundred-yard race. The distance of the race is our lifetime from premortality through life in the spirit world. However, and this is the blessing and surprise, He does not ask us to run against each other. He does not ask us to beat each other. In fact, He asks us to help each other in the race. He knows some can run speedily and some can barely run at all. He only asks that we run to the best of our ability. He has laid out the course perfectly for us. We can only fail if we choose to leave the track.

If we exercise a small amount of faith, that of reading the scriptures, we will receive rewards to strengthen us and give us hope. One aspect of our reward is given to us from God, through John the Revelator. It is a beautiful intimation of what the celestial kingdom is like, given to us in terms that we can understand and images that we can comprehend. This revelation is a glimpse of what a glorious reward our Heavenly Father would have us receive if we but hearken to His will. Yet as glorious as this description is, we can be assured that it will pale in comparison to the reality of the kingdom.

> And he carried me away in the spirit to a great and high
> mountain, and shewed me that great city, the holy Jerusalem,

descending out of heaven from God, having the glory of God: and her light was like unto a stone most precious, even like a jasper stone, clear as crystal; and had a wall great and high, and had twelve gates, and at the gates twelve angels, and names written thereon, which are the names of the twelve tribes of the children of Israel: on the east three gates; on the north three gates; on the south three gates; and on the west three gates.

And the wall of the city had twelve foundations, and in them the names of the twelve apostles of the Lamb. And he that talked with me had a golden reed to measure the city, and the gates thereof, and the wall thereof. And the city lieth foursquare, and the length is as large as the breadth: and he measured the city with the reed, twelve thousand furlongs. The length and the breadth and the height of it are equal.

And he measured the wall thereof, an hundred and forty and four cubits, according to the measure of a man, that is, of the angel. And the building of the wall of it was of jasper: and the city was pure gold, like unto clear glass. And the foundations of the wall of the city were garnished with all manner of precious stones. The first foundation was jasper; the second, sapphire; the third, a chalcedony; the fourth, an emerald; the fifth, sardonyx; the sixth, sardius; the seventh, chrysolite; the eighth beryl; the ninth, a topaz; the tenth, a chrysoprasus; the eleventh, a jacinth; the twelfth, an amerthyst.

And the twelve gates were twelve pearls; every several gate was of one pearl: and the street of the city was pure gold, as it were transparent glass. And I saw no temple therein: for the Lord God Almighty and the Lamb are the temple of it. And the city had no need of the sun, neither of the moon, to shine in it: for the glory of God did lighten it, and the Lamb is the light thereof. And the nations of them which are saved shall walk in the light of it: and the kings of the earth do bring their glory and honour into it.

And the gates of it shall not be shut at all by day: for there shall be no night there. And they shall bring the glory and honour of the nations into it. And there shall in no wise enter into it any thing that defileth, neither whatsoever worketh abomination, or maketh a lie: but they which are written in the Lamb's book of life. (Revelation 21:10–27)

Indescribable beauty, peace, and blessings wait for those of us who live our earthly lives in accordance with the celestial law. The realm of divinity is to sit upon thrones and rule kingdoms and principalities. We may come to embody perfect love and all that it entails. We are promised that if we conform our lives to the will of Heavenly Father by following and obeying the ordinances and laws instituted for our salvation and clearly contained in the scriptures, we may be a joint-heir with Christ and receive all that the Father hath.

To put it simply, it is Heavenly Father's will that we become as He is. As God is, we may become. Through His plan for our happiness, we may rule and reign with Him and Christ for all eternity. We may share their glory and divinity. Christ stated this Himself in both the Old Testament and the New Testament: "I have said, Ye are gods; and all of you are children of the most High" (Psalm 82:6), and, "Jesus answered them, Is it not written in your law, I said, Ye are gods?" (John 10:34).

In the gospel of John, Jesus is rebuking the Jews who were attempting to stone Him. He was pointing out that they should know the law that was given to them as contained in what we now know as the Old Testament. A key element in Christ's statement in both testaments is, "Ye are gods." It must be pointed out and should be obvious that when speaking of Heavenly Father's children, children of the most High, Christ does not mean that they are gods at this time or in times past. Christ's implication is that man has the potential to become a god.

That leads us to examine godhood.

chapter twenty-five

TO BE AS GOD

Jesus answered them, Is it not written in your law, I said, Ye are gods?

—John 10:34

"Ye are gods" is a declarative statement from one who cannot lie. The thought that we may one day share with Christ all that was promised Him and eventually attain parity with Him and Heavenly Father is both thrilling and terrifying—thrilling because of the possibilities and terrifying because of the responsibilities.

At present, we are but young adults in our spiritual development. We attend the University of Temporality. We have passed the initial test presented to us during our premortal schooling and are now engaged in the trials of the proving grounds of earthly endeavor. We have been sent forth from our home and parents to see how well we have learned our premortal lessons and if we will honor the covenants we made at that time. We have been educated from the beginning. We are, at present, still learning, and this will continue throughout our next estate. We must honor the commandments and keep our covenants. We must develop, until we reach perfection, all the attributes of perfect love, for that is the state of godhood.

To be as God is—that is our blessing and our right, predicated upon our faithfulness and actions. But what is it that God does? How does He spend his time? What does He do that we will do and that will define us as gods and goddesses?

For us to examine, understand, and evaluate what that must be like, we must know the character of God. The more we know about Him, the more accurately we may emulate Him, the closer we may be with Him and the mysteries of heaven and the plan of salvation will be more greatly unfolded to us. We will be more effective and capable in serving our fellow man. We will become more profitable servants.

What, then, is this defining quality, character? It is the pattern of behavior. It is personality, moral construct, strength, and constitution. It is essential quality and nature. It is the exhibition or manifestation of those qualities and behavior presented at all times and in all places regardless of what situations arise.

An examination of Heavenly Father's abilities and attributes will help us understand His character.

God has the ability to exercise His omnipotence at will. He has power over the elements and the power to create worlds. He has the power to make worlds pass through the process of exaltation. He has the power of eternal procreation and the power to create mortal bodies for His spirit children. He has power over mortal man's life and death. He has the power of judgment and reward, mercy and punishment, the power to discern man's thoughts and intents and to see all things past, present, and future.

God has the power to know all things and to forgive and pardon. He has the power to hear and answer prayers and to reveal His will. He has the power to determine the bounds of man's habitation and the power to resurrect. He has the power to bind in heaven what is bound on earth. He has the power to institute, organize, and run governments, both in heaven and on earth. He has the power to bless and to heal. He has the power to know all things, past, present, and future.

God has the power of enlightenment, the power to disseminate pure knowledge befitting His needs and that of His children. He has the power of omnipresence. He can receive and answer the prayers of all His children at the same time, yet provide them with total and completely individual attention. He has the power to appoint worthy beings to act in His stead to further advance His kingdom on earth as it is in heaven.

God has the attributes of understanding and compassion, patience and action. He exercises perfect judgment through perfect wisdom. He leads by example and not by force. He is charitable and giving. He allows free will and choice. He is as tender as the demands of justice will allow. He respects no person, yet He respects us all. He is comforting, nurturing, and enlightening. He is perfect in love, and He is perfect in service.

His character defines that which is of most worth, and through His character, He has established the family unit as being definitive of joy and happiness.

The family reigns supreme; it is both the cause and effect of joy. It is the whole that circumscribes all truth. The family sets the parameters for the purpose of existence with exaltation as the goal. The family is alpha and omega, the beginning and end. It is the key and central point of godhood and the purpose for all that has and is yet to transpire.

A beautiful and illuminating story of budding godhood is that of Abraham and his son Isaac.

A paradigm of several salient aspects of godhood is set before us in the covenant established between Heavenly Father and Abraham. This depiction of events is given to us so that we might understand and comprehend the importance of faith, service, and the blessings of, and those received through, an eternal family. It is revelatory as to the foundation upon which rests the purpose of godhood, which is nothing less than the eternal nature of, and godly care for, the family.

Abraham, though not knowing why, dutifully offered up his son Isaac as a sacrifice unto the Lord in obedience to divine commandment. His actions were stayed by the voice of an angel, and a sacrificial ram was provided in the stead of his son.

In this historical record, Abraham is given as a mortal type, or example, of Heavenly Father. Isaac, his son, is a type of Jesus Christ, God's Only Begotten Son. God in his infinite mercy would never demand or accept a human sacrifice from any being. So why was this act proposed to man?

First, what transpired was given to set forth a living example for that current generation, as well as those generations that would follow, of Heavenly Father and His sacrificial lamb, Jesus Christ. Second, so that Abraham's generation, and all succeeding generations, would learn that by putting God first in our life and in giving our lives to Him with trust and in faith, we will receive the greatest blessing God could bestow upon us—the Abrahamic covenant. For the correct perspective pertaining to this covenant, we must remember that Abraham and Sarah were married after the manner of God's law, which decreed that marriage was to be not only for time but throughout all eternity as well. What follows is the Abrahamic covenant:

> And the angel of the Lord called unto Abraham out of heaven the second time, and said, By myself have I sworn, saith the Lord, for because thou hast done this thing, and hast not withheld thy son, thine only son: That in blessing I will bless thee, and in multiplying I will multiply thy seed as the stars of the heaven, and as

the sand which is upon the sea shore; and thy seed shall possess the gate of his enemies; and in thy seed shall all the nations of the earth be blessed; because thou hast obeyed by voice. (Genesis 22:15–18)

Abraham was blessed to stand as the father of an endless posterity for all eternity. As Abraham is a type of God, and God has and does beget spirit children, so it is given as a covenant with Abraham to do likewise. Abraham's children will be more numerous than the stars in the heavens or the sands upon the shores.

The recital of this event is given to us that we might understand that we too may receive this ultimate blessing. Man and woman may be as God is, as Abraham and Sarah are, and reign over a family that will live in perpetuity.

There is no mistake or coincidence that this example is given at the beginning of the Bible, a wonderful book of instructions. All things build from a foundation. The supernal dictate is that the family reigns supreme and all that should emanate from our actions should be for the reverence, protection, and preservation of this eternal unit. Certainly, our Father's greatest sacrifice was for the preservation of the family. "For God so loved the world, that he gave his only begotten Son, that whosoever beliveth in him shall not perish, but have everlasting life" (John 3:16). As the Atonement was a selfless act of perfect love and service, how much more so was the gift of His Son.

It is unimaginable that during mortality we would sacrifice one of our children, nor that God would truly have us so do. Heavenly Father's acquiescence to the sacrifice of His son was done with divine understanding, knowledge, and authority, and not done to appease some imaginary god or idol. God sacrificed His Son that He might have that Son back again and that the gate to heavenly exaltation would be opened to us all. Even taking into account Christ's voluntary volition and its mitigating effect upon the pain our Father must have felt, how terrible must have been God's suffering.

Yet, despite Godly suffering, joy and happiness beyond compare awaits future gods and goddesses. This joy and happiness comes with a depth of experience and meaning that our finite minds are unable to imagine. There is a limit to the speculation and reasoning powers of temporal souls but not that of God. With godhood, the limits are removed. Reasoning, events, moments, thoughts, occurrences, and all the things that make up life are experienced to their infinite and complete fulness. There is perfection in all that we do and experience. Perfect completeness is the complement of being god.

We have been given, here in mortality, a perfect opportunity to understand, within the limitations imposed upon us by temporal life, what it is like to be a god or goddess. It is given to us in the form of our mortal family. We stand at the head of a finite posterity; God at the head of endless posterity. We exercise our authority over our family imperfectly, whereas God makes no mistakes. We love our spouses and children, and yet we know we could love them better and more. We guide and instruct with what we hope to be wisdom and love, yet personal prejudices and preferences, our inherent lack of abilities and knowledge, and our imperfect motives all serve to color our dominion. We are simply unable to rule and reign over our mortal families with the clarity that comes with the perfection of godhood. Yet, what a perfect testing ground and trial experience for us to have to take into the eternities. On earth we are a demigod over our family, with our mistakes to give us, and them, experience. Experience to shape and mold and begin to form us into perfect people. What a blessing that the mistakes we make need not follow us into eternity. We are agents unto ourselves and have the gift of repentance and the gift of divine guidance to assuage the erroneous choices we have made in our lives and will continue to make upon the road to perfection.

As we reign imperfectly during mortality, God reigns perfectly in eternity. In our homes, mother bakes the pies. Out in the backyard, daughter bakes the mud pies. Someday the experiences gained making mud pies will transform into the ability to make apple pies. So it is with governing a mortal family. We will rise in understanding, through experience, until we will be able to get it right. Only then will we be entrusted to stand at the head of an endless posterity, as does Heavenly Father. How horrible it would be if our imperfect choices followed us throughout eternity. How wonderful it is that God will not allow us to attain godhood with the possibility of that happening.

We must reach perfection in charity and compassion, empathy and understanding. We must be perfect in judgment as well as in showing mercy.

But most of all, to be as God is, to become perfect love, we must be perfect in service. There was no greater act of love and no greater act of service shown to mankind than the Atonement of our Savior, Jesus Christ. The verity of the magnitude of this act is substantiated in John

15:13, which reads: "Greater love hath no man than this, that a man lay down his life for his friends."

Our Exemplar showed us the way by laying down His life for us. He has shown us not only the way to God but also the way to be a god. The Atonement was an act of ultimate service. It served Heavenly Father's purpose, that being the opening of the gateway whereby we might return unto Him, and it served us by providing the opportunity to become like Him.

There has been no greater gift, no act of greater selflessness, than the Atonement. It was freely provided for us. How truly humbled we should feel and how completely devoted we should be. How terrible it would be for us to turn our back to this act of grace and mercy.

To be a god is not an easy task. It is not an existence of endless repose. It is so much more than sitting upon a throne and receiving eternal praise and adoration and being the recipient of servitude. God is our master in that He is all-powerful and has provided for us all that we have. God is our servant, because He uses His mastery only for our benefit. His power is exercised not in a capacity of control, domination, or predestination but rather in His desire to serve us. The greatest is he that is the least.

To be as God is is to be the perfect servant. It is to serve one and all. It is to devote oneself to an eternity of selfless dedication to the welfare and advancement of our children. It is to stand by and watch as loved ones make choices that are proper and correct or improper and incorrect. It is to watch them make choices that will affect their eternal existence.

There are some in mortality who have had the most unfortunate experience of having their children choose to disappear, never to know if they are alive or dead, never to see them again. There are some who have had to ask their children to leave home. These parents experience daily pain and anguish over the separation and loss of their loved one. With eons during eternity with which to populate His heavenly kingdom, God our Father lost fully one-third of His children to the enticings of Satan. Heavenly Father knows where these children are, yet because of their choices and the resulting consequences, He will never be reunited with them again. Those poor brothers and sisters of ours will be lost from contact with God and us for the rest of eternity. The influence of one pretentious, arrogant, and egotistical sibling had such a devastating effect over so many. How very sad it is to lose a sibling. How terribly sad it is to lose a child. How horrendously sad to lose as many as our Father has. To have a depletion within our families is a most trying experience, filled with deep anguish.

Everything that pertains to godhood is intrinsically and inextricably interwoven within the family unit and all that pertains to society. With God, all societies, nations, and worlds are simply realms that He has provided for His children to inhabit.

So it is given that to be as God is, we must have total and complete knowledge of everything that affects and provides life for our family throughout eternity. We must provide them with a place to live, and as procreation is eternal, that will require worlds without end.

In the movie *Contact*, the question of the possibility of life on other planets was posed. A most insightful reply was given: "If there wasn't, it would be an awful waste of space." Heavenly Father is not wasteful.

When we are gods and goddesses, we will exercise perfect love, which includes judgment and justice as well as mercy. We will teach our children all that they must know during their premortal estate to educate them as to all situations, possibilities, events, and outcomes that will occur in mortality and beyond and then allow them to stand on their own, to choose for themselves whether to follow our guiding advice and instruction. We must not leave them completely alone, for the forces of evil and temptation will be too overwhelming to be borne without assistance, so we must provide omniscient instruction through chosen people and personal communication through prayer and revelation. We will provide the means of repentance and the gift of an atonement. We will nurture, love, guide, instruct, encourage, and discipline them.

Being a god or goddess carries a great and awesome responsibility. Unlimited power exercised as you work tirelessly toward the goal of your children returning to live with you, while never doing anything to the detriment of other beings or elements. To be a god or a goddess is to never seek benefit for yourself: not riches, thrones, principalities, dominions, kingdoms, omniscience, omnipresence, or omnipotence, no rank or glory or to be worshiped. To be god is to be the ultimate and quintessential servant. It is to be the paradigm of humble servitude.

Did Christ shirk His task in Gethsemane or seek to satisfy His ego through the Atonement? Clearly, His statement, "Not my will, but thine, be done" signifies His complete subjugation to divine wisdom. He served His Father and served us with no thought of Himself.

Let us touch upon supernal attributes of service.

A servant is someone who provides when asked or commanded. A good servant is one who anticipates needs, prepares for that which is to come, handles situations as they occur, and provides for what is to take place in the future and does so without command. A perfect servant does all of the above with no thought of personal gain; his only care and desire is for the betterment of his master.

Let us begin to place ourselves in the position of a god.

The key to godhood is celestial marriage. In other words, marriage that is ordained for all time and eternity. Eternal marriage sets the proper order and moral bounds for family life. It is the everlasting commitment between a man and a woman where the two may join and become one flesh. They are equal. They become one in purpose and will, desire, and hope. This holy union allows gods and goddesses to function with one goal in mind—the continuation and exaltation of an eternal family unit.

With marriage comes children, and as Heavenly Father had spirit children, so shall we. In time, we will have spirit children as numerous as the sands of the seashores, in accordance with the Abrahamic covenant. The time will come when our spirit children will need a place of mortality where they can be tested and tried as we were. They will need worlds to inhabit and care for.

We must provide means for our progeny that are of an eternal nature. The laws that govern salvation, exaltation, the priesthood, and the kingdoms of God have been decreed and instituted from the beginning. We simply continue to educate and train our spirit children to grow in righteousness in the manner that was prescribed and set forth by our Heavenly Father. We educate them in the plan of salvation with all that it entails. We prepare them for the essential and necessary trials they will need to undergo in mortality, that they might exercise their agency in accordance with holy declaration and edict. We prepare them to live a mortal life by faith and provide them with the blessing of repentance. Just as we do with our children now, we ready them to live away from our presence. From among them a Savior must be chosen, as well as prophets and leaders. They will need a comforter. Our spirit children will need all that was provided for us to facilitate our growth and progression.

As a god, we will be blessed to have an endless and eternal posterity. This will necessitate endless worlds. It will be our responsibility to organize the eternal elements into planets, moons, stars, and galaxies. It will be our duty to form worlds that will support temporal life. We will also establish realms for hell, the spirit prison, paradise, and the degrees of heaven.

We will do all things Heavenly Father has done to perpetuate the family unit in glory and exaltation.

This is Father's will for us.

When we think of endless posterity, even our comparatively weak mortal reasoning tells us that simple space requirements demand a multiplicity of worlds. Stating this as fact, the Bible is quite clear on the subject: "God, who at sundry times and in divers manners spake in time past unto the fathers by the prophets, hath in these last days spoken unto us by his Son, whom he hath appointed heir of all things, by whom also he made the worlds" (Hebrews 1:1–2).

Worlds. Plural. Not stars or planets or moons. Not just the earth, the name given to this world, but worlds. Worlds are populated. God commands us to reason together. It is given to common sense, as Heavenly Father is the author of all the physical laws, worlds without end are necessary and can and have been organized for His children without end.

So it will be for us.

We will be responsible for the mountains and seas, the lakes and rivers, the birds and all animals with which we wish to populate the worlds. We will organize the heavens and all things in them. We will make man and woman in our image, as we have been made in the image of our Heavenly Parents.

We will watch over all our children at all times and in all ways. We will serve them in perfection and love. We will guide them and bless them with agency. We will nurture them and chastise them when necessary. We will teach them as we have been taught and love them as we have been loved.

In our exaltation, we will rule as kings and queens, priests and priestesses. We will have dominion over nations, principalities, kingdoms, worlds, and heavens. We will deliver all glory to Christ, who in turn delivers it to Heavenly Father. We will share all with Christ. We will be crowned with ethereal glory as our Father before us.

Yet, as our Heavenly Father possesses all, He gives it all away. Christ is His heir, and an heir is one who receives. What Christ has done with His gift and all others that He will receive is to give them back to His Father. It is a continual process of giving and receiving and never taking. That is what transpires between the Father and the Son and between Father and us. It is also what will transpire between our children and ourselves.

In our glorious exaltation, we will possess all and we will possess nothing. We will not be trapped in the web of endless acquisition. We will be free from all encumbrances and live to serve our Father and our children and each other with all our heart, might, mind, and strength.

We will become perfect love and perfect servants.

As God is, we may become.

GLOSSARY

Agency: The freedom, gift, and blessing to make our own choices of our own volition.

Atonement: The act performed by Christ to make reparations for the sins of mankind.

Baptism: From the Greek *baptisma,* meaning to immerse [in water].

Baptism for the dead: Carrying out the principles and ordinances necessary for salvation, performed in behalf of those who are dead; of those who never had the opportunity to learn of those ordinances and have passed away. Baptism, conferring the Holy Ghost, etc., are performed by proxy here on earth for those in the spirit world.

Celestial glory: This is the glory of God and Jesus Christ. This is the third degree of heaven, of which the Apostle Paul speaks. This is the heaven that we are promised as a joint-heir with Christ if we but obey the gospel principles and ordinances. Celestial glory shines as the sun. In the celestial kingdom sit the rulers of kingdoms, thrones, and principalities.

It is from this kingdom, and only this kingdom, that we may have an eternal increase as promised in the Abrahamic covenant.

Comforter: The Holy Ghost.

Damnation: To have our spiritual progression stopped because of how we exercised our moral agency.

Damned: To never again be in the presence of God.

Death: The separation of our spirit and our physical body.

Degrees of glory: Each of the three heavens, the telestial, terrestrial, and celestial has its own particular glory, likened to the brightness of the stars, moon, and sun.

Eternal life: In its most simplistic form, eternal life is nothing more that living forever, or immortality. It is sometimes used synonymously with exaltation.

Exaltation: By conforming our life to the principles and ordinances required by Heavenly Father, we may be exalted as is Christ. Exaltation is to live in the presence of God and Jesus Christ for all eternity, to be a joint-heir with Christ and to have a life throughout eternity as theirs.

First death: The separation of our spirit and our physical body.

First estate: Where we lived with Heavenly Father in the premortal existence.

First principles of the gospel: The first principle of the gospel is faith. The second is repentance.

Gift of the Holy Ghost: The right given to those who have undertaken the necessary principles and performed the necessary ordinances as set forth by God, to have the constant companionship of the Holy Ghost. This gift is efficacious as long as we remain worthy.

God the Father: Elohim, the first member of the Godhead. He is the father of our spirits. He is the supreme ruler. He is all-knowing, all-powerful, and the embodiment of perfect love. Under His direction, all things were created by Jehovah, who, in mortality, is Jesus Christ.

Grace: The love, mercy, and condescension of God.

Heaven: The residence of God.

Heavenly reward: The kingdom where we will spend eternity as determined by how we lived our mortal lives and exercised our agency in the spirit world. There are three rewards or heavens provided for the various degrees of obedience to God's laws.

Hell: To be separated from the presence of God. The second death. That portion of the spirit world reserved for those who led mortal lives counter to the laws of God. Also, outer darkness.

Holy Ghost: The third member of the Godhead. A personage of spirit. His purpose is to testify to us of the truthfulness of things. These promptings are not to be confused with the gift of the Holy Ghost. Also called the Comforter, the Holy Spirit of Truth, the Holy Spirit. Prayers to God are offered in the name of Christ. The answers are related by the prompting of the Holy Ghost. This prompting is generally an impression in our mind; a still, small voice; a warmth in our breast; and so on. It is never wild excitement. The testimony of the Holy Ghost is manifested in a still, quiet, and peaceful manner.

Immortality: To live forever. This free gift, brought about by the Atonement, is given to everyone who kept their first estate.

Jesus Christ: Jehovah of the Old Testament. The God of Abraham, Isaac, and Jacob. The Son of God and His Only Begotten in the flesh. Christ is our elder brother. Christ performed the atoning sacrifice for mankind. He overcame sin in the Garden of Gethsemene, and He overcame death on the cross at Golgotha. He created the worlds while still a spirit under the direction of our Heavenly Father.

Judgment: Our consignment to one of the three degrees of heaven or outer darkness. We will be rewarded according to our works performed in accordance to the laws and commandments established by God.

Keeping our first estate: The choice we made in the premortal life to follow God's plan of happiness and salvation. Those who chose to follow Lucifer "kept not their first estate" and were cast out from heaven, our presence and the presence of God. One of the many consequences of their choice was to be denied a physical body.

Lucifer: The name of he who rebelled against God's plan and influenced one-third of Heavenly Father's children, our brothers and sisters, to follow his lead. Like Christ, Lucifer was also our elder brother.

Mercy: The act of intercession by Christ to lessen our suffering and still satisfy justice. The love of God manifested by judging us as leniently as possible and still fulfilling the demands of justice.

Outer darkness: The final place of eternal habitation for Satan and Cain, those spirit children who kept not their first estate, and other sons of perdition who commit the unpardonable sin.

Paradise: That portion of the spirit world reserved for those who lived mortal lives in accordance with God's laws. It is a place of rest from the pains of mortality, where the righteous reside prior to resurrection and judgment. Nevertheless, much work will be done to carry forth the plan of salvation to those who did not have the opportunity to receive those teachings in mortality.

Premortal: The era prior to the birth of our physical bodies.

Premortal existence: Our life as spirit children comprising our first estate spent in the presence of our Heavenly Father.

Resurrection: The reuniting of our spirits and our physical bodies. This takes place after mortal death and prior to our judgment.

Salvation: When Christ overcame the effects of sin and physical death, the gift of salvation was presented in the form of immortality to everyone who kept their first estate. This is a general salvation given to all by the grace of God. Also called salvation by grace or mercy. Salvation does not automatically grant us the blessings of exaltation and eternal life.

Satan: The name given to Lucifer upon being cast out of the spirit world.

Second Comforter: Jesus Christ.

Second death: To be separated from the presence of God and Christ.

Second estate: Our mortal life.

Spirit, spirit body: Our spirit, or spirit body, houses our intelligence. It is "who we are." It is in the personage of our body, although independent of our body.

Spirit children: We are the literal and actual offspring of God. We are His children. He is the Father of our Spirits; hence we are His spirit children.

Spirit world, spirit prison: The place of our habitation after our mortal death and prior to our eternal reward in one of the three degrees of heaven. It is divided into paradise and hell.

Telestial glory/telestial kingdom: The lowest glory and

kingdom in heaven. All who kept their first estate will not be blessed with some form of reward. In this case, the telestial is the least of all rewards. It is reserved for those who lived a telestial law in mortality, that being those that are sensual, carnal, devilish, murderers, thieves, liars, cheats, etc. There is no progression to a higher reward, and the Abrahamic promise is withheld from them. The earth is now in a telestial state.

Terrestrial glory: The kingdom and degree of glory above the telestial and below the celestial kingdoms, described as having a glory comparable to that of the moon. This glory is brighter than the stars yet dimmer than the sun. This is a state of paradisical glory, the state the world was in prior to Adam and Eve being cast out of the Garden of Eden. This kingdom is reserved for those honorable people who fail to partake of the principles and ordinances necessary for exaltation. There is no progression to a higher reward, and the Abrahamic promise is withheld from them.

Unpardonable sin: The sin against the Holy Ghost. Those few people who have been blessed to have a sure testimony of God, Christ, and the Holy Ghost and then actively work to deny that knowledge and lead others away from the truth have committed the unpardonable sin.

Veil: Often called the veil of forgetfulness. This is the forgetting or clouding within our minds of the events we experienced during our first estate. Its purpose is so that, during our mortal sojourn, we may exercise our freedom of choice, or agency, based completely upon faith.

SOURCES

Crowther, Duane S. *Life Everlasting: A Definitive Study of Life after Death.* Bountiful, Utah: Horizon Publishers, 1999.

Journal of Discourses, 26 vols. London: Latter-day Saints' Book Depot, 1854–86.

Kimball, Spencer W. *Faith Precedes the Miracle.* Salt Lake City: Deseret Book, 1972.

Lewis, C. S. *Mere Christianity.* New York: Simon & Schuster, 1980.

McConkie, Bruce R. *Mormon Doctrine.* 2d ed. Salt Lake City: Bookcraft, 1966.

Milton, John. *Paradise Lost.* New York: Penguin Books, 1981.

Nelson, Russell M. *The Gateway We Call Death.* Salt Lake City: Deseret Book, 1995.

Oaks, Dallin H. *The Lord's Way.* Salt Lake City: Deseret Book, 1991.

Pratt, Parley P. *Key to the Science of Theology.* Salt Lake City: Deseret Book, 1973.

Robinson, Stephen E. *Believing Christ.* Salt Lake City: Deseret Book, 1992.

Smith, Joseph. *Teachings of the Prophet Joseph Smith.* Selected by Joseph Fielding Smith. Salt Lake City: Deseret Book, 1976.

Smith, Joseph Fielding. *Answers to Gospel Questions.* Salt Lake City: Deseret Book, 1957.

Talmage, James E. *Jesus The Christ.* Salt Lake City: Deseret Book, 1982.

Top, Brent L. *The Life Before.* Salt Lake City: Deseret Book, 1988.

ABOUT THE AUTHOR

Photo by Vanessa M. Colwell

Steven C. Colwell was born and raised in Los Angeles. Always of a spiritual proclivity, he requested baptism at the age of nine into the Baptist faith. After becoming disillusioned with certain aspects of Baptist beliefs and those of Western religion in general, he took a spiritual journey that incorporated a blend of Buddhism, Taoism, Hinduism, and Western beliefs.

An epiphany in 1992 led him to become a member of The Church of Jesus Christ of Latter-day Saints, which concurred with all that he had intrinsically known was true. In his twelve-year Church membership, he has served in a bishopric, as a high councilor, in the leadership of a high priests group, and in a variety of other Church callings.

Steven and his wife, Charlotte, live in Moreno Valley, California. They are the parents of two children.